P9-BYF-659

Good Housekeeping FAVORITE RECIPES

VEGETARIAN MEALS

HEARST BOOKS
A division of Sterling Publishing Co., Inc.

New York / London
www.sterlingpublishing.com

Rosemary Ellis   **Editor in Chief**

Richard Eisenberg   **Special Projects
Director**

Susan Westmoreland   **Food Director**

Susan Deborah   **Associate Food
Goldsmith   Director**

Delia Hammock   **Nutrition Director**

Sharon Franke   **Food Appliances
Director**

Book Design by Renato Stanisic

Photography Credits:
Quentin Bacon: page 44.
James Baigrie: page 199.
Mary Ellen Bartley: page. 167.
Beatrix Da Costa: pages 65 and 90.
Brian Hagiwara: pages 6, 50, 68, 81, 117, 124, 129,
130, 133, 134, 143, 146, 149, 151, 154, 157, 162,
164, 168, 178, 193, 194, 212, 216, 223, and 231.
Rita Maas: pages 19 and 202.
Alan Richardson: pages 3, 37, 100, 114, 119,
173, 185, 186, 206, and 226.
Ann Stratton: pages 2, 14, 25, 31, 32, 41, 47, 60,
75, 82, 88, 95, and 97.
Mark Thomas: pages 93, 109, 144 and 224.
Jonelle Weaver: pages 8 and 106.

Library of Congress Cataloging-in-
Publication Data

Vegetarian meals : good housekeeping
favorite recipes / the editors of Good
housekeeping.
p. cm.
Includes index.
ISBN 1-58816-516-7
1. Vegetarian cookery. I. Good Housekeeping
(New York, N.Y.)
TX837.V42665 2006
641.5'636--dc22
2005018985

10 9

Published by Hearst Books
A division of Sterling Publishing Co., Inc.
387 Park Avenue South, New York, NY 10016

Good Housekeeping is a registered trademark
of Hearst Communications, Inc.

www.goodhousekeeping.com

For information about custom editions,
special sales, premium and corporate purchases,
please contact Sterling Special Sales
Department at 800-805-5489 or special-
sales@sterlingpublishing.com.

Distributed in Canada by Sterling Publishing
c/o Canadian Manda Group, 165 Dufferin Street
Toronto, Ontario, Canada M6K 3H6

Distributed in Australia by Capricorn Link
(Australia) Pty. Ltd.
P.O. Box 704, Windsor, NSW 2756 Australia

Manufactured in China

Sterling ISBN 978-1-58816-516-9

The Good Housekeeping Triple-Test Promise

We make sure that every recipe that bears the *Good Housekeeping* name works in any oven, with any brand of ingredient, no matter what. That's why, in our test kitchens at the *Good Housekeeping Research Institute,* we test each recipe at least three times—and, often, several more times after that.

When a recipe is first developed one member of our team prepares the dish and we judge it on these criteria: it must be **delicious, family-friendly, healthy,** and **easy-to-make.**

1. The recipe is then tested several times **to fine-tune the flavor** and **ease of preparation,** always by the same team member, using the same equipment.

2. Next, another team member follows the recipe as written, **varying the brands of ingredients** and **kinds of equipment.** Even the types of stoves we use are changed.

3. A third team member repeats the whole process **using yet another set of equipment** and **alternative ingredients.**

By the time our recipes appear on these pages, they are guaranteed to work in any kitchen, including yours. **WE PROMISE.**

Caribbean Black-Bean Soup

CONTENTS

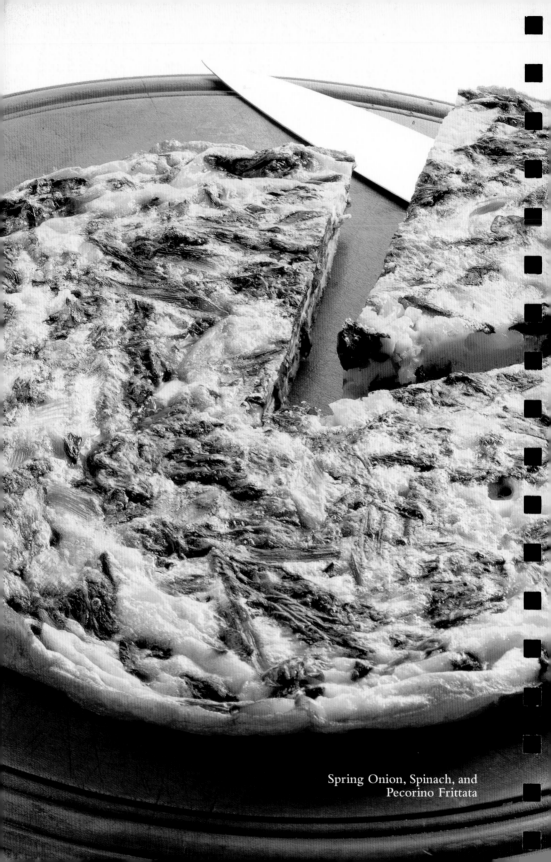

Spring Onion, Spinach, and
Pecorino Frittata

FOREWORD

I cook a lot of meatless dinners these days. Like many of you, I find that I'm not hungry for meat every night and I know that we get more than our fair share of protein. Growing up in an Italian-American family, a frittata, minestrone, and pasta e fagioli were often the main course at dinner, which might have been rounded out with cheese, along with a platter of broccoli drizzled with olive oil and lemon juice, or a simple tossed salad. I always loved these dinners but somehow never thought of them as "vegetarian."

Can a whole book on *Vegetarian Cooking* be real food for real families? Yes. Even if you have only 30 minutes to make dinner for picky eaters? Yes. This collection of over 150 recipes will give you family-friendly weeknight choices that require no mysterious ingredients or complicated techniques. Along with recipes there are tips, shortcuts, and suggestions for rounding out the meal, and some variations on featured recipes. You'll find chapters on Soups and Stews, Lunch and Brunch, Main-Dish Salads, Quick Dinners, and One-Dish Meals—so whatever you're cooking for, we've got you covered. And with these delicious triple-tested selections, we think you'll hear lots exclamations of "Yum!"

—Susan Westmoreland

Food Director, *Good Housekeeping*

Penne with Green Beans
and Basil

INTRODUCTION

For generations, the mealtime mantra of mothers across America has been "Eat your vegetables!" Well, as usual, mother is right. So too are the health professionals who, for decades, have advocated a healthy diet of less meat and more fruits, vegetables, whole grains, lowfat or fat-free dairy products to help us live longer and better.

Americans have finally gotten the message. Tens of millions of people in the U.S. today have changed their eating habits to include more produce and grains and fewer animal products.

While you may not consider yourself a vegetarian, you probably do, in fact, eat a few meatless meals each week. Pancakes for brunch, yogurt and fruit for breakfast, an after-movie pizza with mushrooms and peppers, a quick lunch of vegetable-and-bean burritos, comforting mac-and-cheese casserole or take-out vegetable lo mein for dinner are all satisfying and nutritious fare, yet free of meat, fish, or poultry.

TYPES OF VEGETARIANS

Vegetarians choose to eliminate animal products from their diets for any number of reasons—ethical, environmental, economic, or religious. But according to a recent Gallup Poll, the majority of people who choose to go meatless do so for health reasons. Vegetarians usually fall into one of these groups:

• The **vegan,** or **total vegetarian,** diet includes only foods from plant sources: fruits, vegetables, legumes (dried beans and peas), whole grains, seeds, and nuts.

• The **lactovegetarian** diet includes plant foods plus cheese and other dairy products.

• The **ovo-lactovegetarian** diet is the same as the lactovegetarian, but also includes eggs.

• The **semivegetarian** diet, which is frequently favored by those who are just easing into a vegetarian lifestyle or who want to add more meatless meals to their diet, does not include red meat but does include chicken and fish along with plant foods, dairy products, and eggs.

EATING VEGETARIAN

Good Housekeeping does not advocate a vegetarian diet in *Vegetarian Meals.* Rather, we assembled a collection of our favorite healthful, flavor-packed recipes because, like many of our readers, you want to add more nutritious meatless dishes to your family's meals. Perhaps you have a member of your family who is a vegetarian, or your child has just announced that he or she wants to give up all animal foods. Or you simply want to introduce more vegetables, fruits, whole grains, legumes, and lowfat products into your meals. In these pages, you'll find a veritable garden of tasty, appealing, meat-free dishes to please everyone at your table.

Like life, variety is the key to delicious vegetarian meals. Experiment with the many available grains, legumes, fruits, and vegetables and combine them with several of the vast array of herbs and spices to marry flavors and add punch. You'll discover that the possibilities are endless.

NUTRITIONAL GUIDELINES

The most important consideration for a nutritionally sound vegetarian diet is to consume a variety of foods and in sufficient amounts to meet the caloric and nutritional needs of each individual. If you are incorporating more meatless meals into your family's menus and fewer animal products, there are several nutrients that you need to focus on to be sure everyone is getting an adequate amount, particularly youngsters:

Protein. You don't need to consume meat, fish, or poultry to have enough protein in your diet. Protein needs can easily be met by eating a variety of plant foods. It is not necessary to include specific combinations of foods (such as rice and beans) in the same meal. A mixture of proteins from grains, legumes, seeds, and vegetables eaten throughout the day will provide enough of all the amino acids, the building blocks of protein, your body needs.

Some sources of protein for vegetarians: legumes (dried peas and beans), seeds, nuts and nut butters, soy protein, cheese, milk and yogurt, eggs, grains, and some vegetables.

Iron. An integral part of hemoglobin which carries oxygen in the blood. Vegetarians who eliminate all meat, poultry and seafood (the primary sources of iron) may be prone to an iron deficiency.

Some sources of iron for vegetarians: legumes, dark green leafy vegetables (except spinach), enriched and whole-grain breads and cereals, nuts, and seeds. Cooking foods in cast-iron cookware can also boost their iron content.

Calcium: The major building material for building bones and teeth.

Some sources of calcium for vegetarians: milk and milk products, dark green leafy vegetables (except spinach), calcium-fortified soy products, fortified juices and cereals.

Zinc. Essential for growth and development and proper functioning of the immune system.

Some sources of zinc for vegetarians: legumes, wheat germ, whole grains, nuts, pumpkin and sunflower seeds, milk and milk products.

Vitamin B-12. Essential for formation of red blood cells and proper functioning of the nervous system. Animal products are the only natural food source of this vitamin.

Some sources of B-12 for vegetarians: milk and milk products, eggs, fortified foods and supplements.

THE VEGETARIAN FOOD GROUPS

Adopting a healthful vegetarian or semivegetarian diet is as simple as choosing a variety of different foods daily from among each of the following seven categories. Try any of the suggested recipes.

• **Breads and grains.** Choose whole or unrefined grain products whenever possible or use fortified or enriched cereals. *Recipes:* Wheat-Berry Salad with Spinach, Roasted Vegetables with Arugula and Whole-Wheat Fusili, Barley Vegetable Stew.

• **Vegetables and fruits.** Always try to use the freshest produce you can get. When fresh is not available, opt first for frozen, then canned. Go for the deepest colors for the highest nutritional content: Most dark green leafy vegetables contain calcium and iron. Deep yellow and orange fruits and vegetables are good sources of beta carotene. Veggies and fruits are also rich in potassium, fiber, folic acid, and vitamin C. *Recipes:* Eggplant and Spinach Stacks, Spiced Sweet-Potato Stew, Vegetarian Tortilla Pie.

• **Beans, peas, soy, and other legumes.** Use beans, peas, and other legumes as a main dish or part of a meal often. They are excellent sources of protein, and also contribute zinc, calcium, and iron. *Recipes:* White Bean and Tomatillo Chili, Lentil Shepherd's Pie, Falafel Sandwiches.

• **Dairy products or calcium-rich substitutes.** If using dairy products, select reduced-fat, lowfat, or fat-free varieties whenever possible. *Recipes:* Savory Rice and Ricotta Tart, Nacho Casserole, Eggplant Parmesan.

• **Nuts and seeds.** Eat a variety of nuts and seeds as a snack, on fruit or vegetable salads, or in main dishes. They are a source of protein, zinc, and iron. Don't overdo—they are high in calories.

• **Fats:** Essential in any diet, but ideally, most fats should come from whole plant foods such as nuts, seeds, and avocado. Moderate amounts of plant oils such as olive, canola, and sesame are good choices for cooking or for salad dressings.

• **Eggs.** Because of their high cholesterol content, you may want to limit eggs to three or four a week or consider using commercial egg substitutes, which contain no cholesterol and can be used freely as a protein source. *Recipes:* Leek and Goat Cheese Quiche, Spinach and Jack Cheese Bread Pudding, Mexican Potato Frittata.

PLANNING MEALS

The key to serving delicious vegetarian meals everyone will enjoy is to create dishes that include some of each food group and have a variety of tastes, colors, and textures.

If you're just beginning on the path to more meatless meals, you may find some resistance from the carnivores in your family. Understand that it will take some time for those who are used to thinking of vegetables as side dishes to see them as the main event. Ask everyone to contribute a list of his or her favorite foods. Many dishes that contain meat can be easily modified to make them vegetarian. Chili, stir-fries, and pasta dishes naturally lend themselves to meatless recipes.

In general, plan your meals around one main dish that is vegetable-, bean-, or grain-based. Then add the appropriate go-withs. For example, if your main course is a vegetable tart, accompany it with potato, grain, or corn for a nutritionally complete meal. With a main course of pasta, add a salad and whole-grain bread. A bean-and-vegetable casserole calls for a side of rice pilaf or other grain.

TIPS FOR BUSY PEOPLE

Most of us spend our days on the go: at work, shuttling kids back and forth, shopping, doing chores. Preparing good, wholesome vegetarian meals for your family shouldn't be a burden. Here are a few shortcuts for healthier cooking.

• Plan menus, make lists, then shop.

• Make sure there are plenty of good-quality ingredients on hand for quick and/or last-minute meals such as pastas, canned beans and tomatoes, frozen vegetables, and cheeses.

• Make two big casseroles or a double-batch of a one-pot dish that will feed your family for two nights. Serve with a salad and whole-grain bread.

• On the weekend, do some basic prep work of foods that can be incorporated into meals during the week: Cook up some rice or other grain, make pasta sauce, or cook a pot of beans.

• Get everyone involved in planning, shopping, and preparing meals. That way, they'll be more likely to eat and enjoy the meal. This approach is also a great way to get children started on healthy eating habits.

SOUPS AND STEWS

Curried Sweet-Potato and Lentil Soup

What is it about a steaming pot of soup or a hearty stew, slowly simmering on the stove and filling the house with enticing aromas, that instinctively reminds us of childhood? Possibly it's because carefully prepared soups and stews have come to symbolize the comforts of home. They warm us when the weather turns cold and console us after a trying day.

For busy cooks with families on the go, soups and stews are a godsend. They need minimal prep work, usually just chopping vegetables and measuring the required amounts of liquid, grains, herbs, and spices that go into the pot. Then, depending on the recipe, the whole lot can simmer slowly or quickly on the stove, in the oven, or in a slow cooker. What's more, many taste even better the next day, which means leftovers are sure to be satisfying.

On days when schedules dictate that everyone has to eat dinner at a different time, it's great to know there's a warm pot of something nutritious and flavorful ready for each person to tuck into. And when you find yourself with a few more hungry mouths to feed than you'd counted on, just add some more veggies or beans to the pot or to the accompanying salad, heat up a hearty loaf of bread, and call the gang in for dinner.

So what will it be tonight? How about the comfort of old-fashioned Tomato and Rice Soup or everyone's favorite bistro classic, French Onion Soup? Savor the flavors of the Old South with Red Bean and Collard Gumbo. Heed the call of the Southwest with any one of our four vegetarian chili recipes. If the exotic appeals to you, try the spicy Thai Coconut Soup or Curried Vegetable Stew, redolent with Indian spices, raisins, and tomatoes.

And lest you think soups and stews are winter-only meals, while you're firing up the outdoor grill, sit down to the refreshing Chilled Buttermilk-Vegetable Soup.

When dinner's done, if you're lucky enough to have even a little bit of leftovers, freeze them in individual-serving size containers to re-heat for a quick meal. Even smaller amounts can serve as an accompaniment to a sandwich or salad.

Stovetop Chili

A quick weeknight chili that's packed with buttery black soybeans, tender-crisp green beans, and melt-in-your-mouth sweet potatoes. Serve with a chunk of warm corn bread.

Prep: 20 minutes   Cook: 35 minutes
Makes about 11 cups or 6 main-dish servings.

1 tablespoon olive oil
1 medium onion, chopped
2 tablespoons chili powder
1 teaspoon ground cumin
1 teaspoon ground coriander
2 garlic cloves, crushed with
  garlic press
1 jalapeño chile, seeded and minced
1 can (28 ounces) whole tomatoes
1/2 pound green beans, trimmed and
  each cut crosswise in half

3 medium sweet potatoes (about
  1 1/2 pounds), peeled and cut
  into 1 1/2-inch pieces
1 teaspoon sugar
1 teaspoon salt
2 cups water
2 cans (15 ounces) black soybeans
  or black beans, rinsed and drained
sour cream (optional)

1. In nonstick 5- to 6-quart Dutch oven, heat oil over medium heat until hot. Add onion and cook, stirring occasionally, until tender, about 10 minutes. Add chili powder, cumin, coriander, garlic, and jalapeño; cook, stirring, 1 minute.

2. Add tomatoes with their juice, green beans, sweet potatoes, sugar, salt, and water; heat to boiling over medium-high heat, breaking up tomatoes with side of spoon. Reduce heat to low; cover and simmer, stirring occasionally, until sweet potatoes are tender, about 25 minutes.

3. Add soybeans and heat through, about 2 minutes longer. Serve with sour cream, if you like.

Each serving: About 275 calories, 14g protein, 45g carbohydrate, 5g total fat (1g saturated), 0mg cholesterol, 635mg sodium.

Vegetarian Chili

Black soybeans, sold in convenient cans, have a better texture and flavor than the usual beige variety and add extra oomph to winter chili.

PREP: 30 MINUTES   COOK: 50 MINUTES
MAKES ABOUT 10 CUPS OR 6 MAIN-DISH SERVINGS.

4 teaspoons olive oil
1 medium butternut squash (about 2 pounds), peeled and cut into ³/₄-inch pieces
3 medium carrots, peeled and cut into ¹/₄-inch pieces
1 large onion (12 ounces), chopped
2 tablespoons chili powder
2 garlic cloves, crushed with garlic press

1 can (28 ounces) plum tomatoes
3 jalapeño chiles, seeded and minced
1 cup vegetable broth
1 tablespoon sugar
¹/₂ teaspoon salt
2 cans (15 ounces each) black soybeans, rinsed and drained
1 cup lightly packed fresh cilantro leaves, chopped
plain nonfat yogurt (optional)

1. In nonstick 5-quart Dutch oven or saucepot, heat 2 teaspoons oil over medium-high heat until hot. Add squash and cook, stirring occasionally, until golden, 8 to 10 minutes. Transfer squash to bowl; set aside.

2. In same Dutch oven, heat remaining 2 teaspoons oil. Add carrots and onion and cook, stirring occasionally, until golden, about 10 minutes. Stir in chili powder and garlic; cook, stirring, 1 minute longer.

3. Add tomatoes with their juice, jalapeños, broth, sugar, and salt; heat to boiling over medium-high heat, stirring to break up tomatoes with side of spoon. Stir in soybeans and squash; heat to boiling over medium-high heat. Reduce heat to low; cover and simmer until squash is tender, about 30 minutes.

4. Remove Dutch oven from heat; stir in cilantro. Serve chili with yogurt, if you like.

Each serving: About 265 calories, 15g protein, 40g carbohydrate, 6g total fat (1g saturated), 0mg cholesterol, 480mg sodium.

Vegetarian Chili

Meatless Chili

So thick and hearty, you'll never miss the meat. Serve by the bowlful, with warm tortillas.

PREP: 30 MINUTES PLUS SOAKING BEANS   BAKE: 1 HOUR 30 MINUTES
MAKES ABOUT 12 1/2 CUPS OR 6 MAIN-DISH SERVINGS.

1 1/2 pounds mixed dry beans, such
   as red kidney, white kidney
   (cannellini), and black
   (3 cups total)
1 tablespoon vegetable oil
3 medium carrots, peeled and cut
   crosswise into 1/4-inch-thick slices
2 medium onions, finely chopped
1 stalk celery, finely chopped
1 medium red pepper, finely chopped
3 garlic cloves, minced

1 jalapeño chile, minced
2 teaspoons ground cumin
1/2 teaspoon ground coriander
1 can (28 ounces) tomatoes in puree
1 chipotle chile in adobo, minced
2 teaspoons salt
1/4 teaspoon dried oregano
1 package (10 ounces) frozen
   whole-kernel corn
1 1/4 cups loosely packed fresh
   cilantro leaves and stems, chopped

1. Place beans in colander and pick through, discarding any stones or debris. Rinse beans with cold running water and drain. Transfer beans to large bowl. Add enough *water* to cover by 2 inches. Cover and let stand at room temperature overnight. (Or, in 5-quart Dutch oven or saucepot, combine beans and enough *water* to cover by 2 inches; heat to boiling over high heat. Boil 2 minutes. Remove from heat; cover and let stand 1 hour.) Drain and rinse beans.

2. Preheat oven to 375°F. In 5-quart Dutch oven, combine beans and *8 cups water;* heat to boiling over high heat. Cover and bake, stirring occasionally, until beans are tender, about 1 hour. Drain beans and return to Dutch oven.

3. Meanwhile, in 10-inch skillet, heat vegetable oil over medium heat until hot. Add carrots, onions, celery, and red pepper; cook, stirring frequently, until vegetables are tender, about 10 minutes. Stir in garlic,

jalapeño, cumin, and coriander; cook, stirring, 30 seconds. Stir in tomatoes with their puree, chipotle chile, salt, and oregano, breaking up tomatoes with side of spoon; heat to boiling over high heat. Reduce heat to low; simmer, uncovered, 10 minutes.

4. Stir tomato mixture, corn, and *2 cups water* into beans; cover and bake 30 minutes longer. Remove Dutch oven from oven; stir in cilantro.

Each serving: About 360 calories, 20g protein, 66g carbohydrate, 4g total fat (0g saturated), 0mg cholesterol, 1,195mg sodium.

White Bean and Tomatillo Chili

A spicy vegetarian chili with fresh tomatillos—tart, green, tomatolike fruits (with papery husks) that are staples in Southwestern cuisine. For this recipe, we used canned, not dry, white kidney beans. Serve with warm tortillas and a dollop of plain yogurt.

PREP: 5 MINUTES   COOK: 25 MINUTES
MAKES ABOUT 9 CUPS OR 4 MAIN-DISH SERVINGS.

2 tablespoons olive oil
3 garlic cloves, crushed with
  garlic press
1 small onion, cut in half and
  thinly sliced
1 jalapeño chile, seeded and minced
1 teaspoon ground cumin
1 pound tomatillos, husked, rinsed,
  and coarsely chopped
1 1/4 teaspoons salt
1/2 teaspoon sugar

1 can (14 1/2 ounces) vegetable broth
  (1 3/4 cups)
1 can (4 ounces) chopped mild
  green chiles, drained
1 cup water
2 cans (15 to 19 ounces each) white
  kidney beans (cannellini), rinsed,
  drained, and coarsely mashed
1 cup loosely packed fresh
  cilantro leaves, chopped

1. In nonstick 10-inch skillet, heat oil over medium heat until hot. Add garlic, onion, jalapeño, and cumin, and cook, stirring often, until light golden, 7 to 10 minutes.
2. Meanwhile, in 5- to 6-quart saucepot, combine tomatillos, salt, sugar, broth, green chiles, and water; heat to boiling over high heat. Reduce heat to low. Stir in onion mixture; cover and simmer 15 minutes.
3. Stir in beans and cilantro; heat through.

Each serving: About 335 calories, 13g protein, 50g carbohydrate, 10g total fat (1g saturated), 0mg cholesterol, 1,610mg sodium.

Cranberry Bean Soup

A Chilean-style soup made with butternut squash, tomatoes, fresh basil, and jalapeño. Cranberry beans have large, knobby beige pods speckled with red; the beans inside are cream-colored with red streaks and have a nutlike taste.

PREP: 40 MINUTES   COOK: 45 MINUTES
MAKES ABOUT 9 CUPS OR 4 MAIN-DISH SERVINGS.

4 teaspoons olive oil
1 medium butternut squash
  (2 pounds), peeled and cut into
  3/4-inch pieces
1 medium onion, chopped
2 garlic cloves, minced
1 jalapeño chile, seeded and minced
1 teaspoon ground cumin
1 can (141/2 ounces) vegetable broth
  (13/4 cups)

2 medium tomatoes, chopped
11/2 pounds fresh cranberry beans,
  shelled (about 2 cups beans)
1 teaspoon salt
1 teaspoon sugar
11/4 cups loosely packed fresh
  basil leaves, chopped
21/4 cups water
2 cups corn kernels cut from cobs
  (about 4 medium ears)

1. In 5-quart Dutch oven, heat 2 teaspoons oil over medium heat until hot. Add squash and onion and cook, stirring occasionally, until golden, about 10 minutes. Transfer squash mixture to bowl.

2. In same Dutch oven, heat remaining 2 teaspoons olive oil over medium heat; add garlic, jalapeño, and cumin and cook, stirring, 1 minute. Stir in broth, tomatoes, beans, salt, sugar, squash mixture, 1/4 cup basil, and water; heat to boiling over high heat. Reduce heat to low; cover and simmer, stirring occasionally, until beans are tender, about 30 minutes.

3. Stir in corn; heat to boiling over high heat. Reduce heat to low; cover and simmer 5 minutes longer. Stir in remaining 1 cup chopped basil.

Each serving: About 353 calories, 15g protein, 68g carbohydrate, 7g total fat (1g saturated), 0mg cholesterol, 854mg sodium.

Caribbean Black Bean Soup

Our new take on black bean soup is made with allspice, thyme, and brown sugar for authentic island flair.

PREP: 45 MINUTES PLUS SOAKING BEANS   COOK: 2 HOURS 30 MINUTES
MAKES ABOUT 13 CUPS OR 6 MAIN-DISH SERVINGS.

1 pound dry black beans
2 tablespoons vegetable oil
2 medium red onions, chopped
4 jalapeño chiles, seeded and minced
2 tablespoons minced, peeled
  fresh ginger
4 garlic cloves, minced
1/2 teaspoon ground allspice
1/2 teaspoon dried thyme
8 cups water

2 medium sweet potatoes (about 12
  ounces each), peeled and cut into
  3/4-inch pieces
1 tablespoon dark brown sugar
2 teaspoons salt
1 bunch green onions, trimmed and
  thinly sliced
1 cup lightly packed fresh
  cilantro leaves, chopped
2 limes, cut into wedges (optional)

1. Place beans in colander and pick through, discarding any stones or debris. Rinse beans with cold running water and drain. Transfer beans to large bowl. Add enough *water* to cover by 2 inches. Cover and let stand at room temperature overnight. (Or, in 5-quart Dutch oven or saucepot, combine beans and enough *water* to cover by 2 inches; heat to boiling over high heat. Boil 2 minutes. Remove from heat; cover and let stand 1 hour.) Drain and rinse beans.

2. In 6-quart saucepot, heat vegetable oil over medium heat until hot. Add onions and cook, stirring occasionally, until tender, about 10 minutes. Add jalapeños, ginger, garlic, allspice, and thyme and cook, stirring, 3 minutes.

3. Add beans and water; heat to boiling over high heat. Reduce heat to low; cover and simmer 1 hour 30 minutes.

4. Add sweet potatoes, brown sugar, and salt; heat to boiling over high heat. Reduce heat to low; cover and simmer until beans and sweet potatoes are tender, about 30 minutes longer.

5. Transfer 1 cup bean mixture to blender; cover, with center part of cover removed to let steam escape, and puree until smooth. Return to saucepot. Stir in green onions and cilantro. Serve with lime wedges, if you like.

Each serving: About 390 calories, 17g protein, 70g carbohydrate, 6g total fat (1g saturated), 0mg cholesterol, 705mg sodium.

Caribbean Black Bean Soup

Vegetarian Lentil Stew

With ready-made soup as its base and precut squash, this hearty Indian-spiced stew is a breeze to prepare.

PREP: 10 MINUTES   COOK: 20 MINUTES
MAKES ABOUT 6 1/4 CUPS OR 4 MAIN-DISH SERVINGS.

2 teaspoons olive oil
2 teaspoons grated, peeled
  fresh ginger
2 garlic cloves, crushed with
  garlic press
2 teaspoons curry powder
1 package (1 pound) precut peeled
  butternut squash (about 4 cups),
  cut into bite-size pieces

1 large apple, unpeeled, cored,
  and cut into 1-inch pieces
1 can (19 ounces) ready-to-serve
  lentil soup
1/4 teaspoon salt
1 cup water
1 bag (10 ounces) prewashed
  spinach
lavash or pita, toasted (optional)

1. In 4-quart saucepan, heat oil over medium heat until hot. Add ginger, garlic, and curry powder, and cook, stirring, 30 seconds. Add squash, apple, soup, salt, and water; cover and heat to boiling over high heat. Reduce heat to medium; cook, covered, until squash is just tender, about 5 minutes longer, stirring occasionally.

2. In batches, gently add as many spinach leaves as will fit in the saucepan to lentil mixture, stirring until spinach has wilted. Cover and simmer gently 5 minutes. Serve stew with lavash, if you like.

Each serving: About 190 calories, 9g protein, 34g carbohydrate, 4g total fat (0g saturated), 0mg cholesterol, 650mg sodium.

Black Bean Soup

For extra south-of-the-border flavor, serve this shortcut soup with thinly sliced pickled jalapeño peppers and crumbled *queso fresco.*

PREP: 10 MINUTES   COOK: 20 MINUTES
MAKES ABOUT 6 1/2 CUPS OR 4 MAIN-DISH SERVINGS.

1 tablespoon vegetable oil
1 medium onion, finely chopped
2 garlic cloves, crushed with
  garlic press
2 teaspoons chili powder
1 teaspoon ground cumin
1/4 teaspoon crushed red pepper
2 cans (16 to 19 ounces each) black
  beans, rinsed and drained

1 can (14 1/2 ounces) vegetable broth
  (1 3/4 cups)
2 cups water
1/2 cup loosely packed fresh
  cilantro leaves, chopped
lime wedges

1. In 3-quart saucepan, heat oil over medium heat until hot. Add onion and cook until tender, about 5 minutes. Stir in garlic, chili powder, cumin, and crushed red pepper; cook 30 seconds. Stir in beans, broth, and water; heat to boiling over high heat. Reduce heat to low; simmer, uncovered, 15 minutes.

2. Spoon half of mixture into blender; cover, with center part of cover removed to let steam escape, and puree until almost smooth. Pour into medium bowl. Repeat with remaining mixture.

3. Return soup to saucepan; heat through. Sprinkle with cilantro and serve with lime wedges.

Each serving: About 265 calories, 22g protein, 46g carbohydrate, 6g total fat (1g saturated), 0mg cholesterol, 965mg sodium.

Lentil and Macaroni Soup

This flavorful and filling soup, chock-full of vegetables, lentils, and pasta, needs only some crusty bread to become a meal. And there's enough to enjoy another day.

PREP: 20 MINUTES   COOK: 50 MINUTES
MAKES ABOUT 12 CUPS OR 6 MAIN-DISH SERVINGS.

1 tablespoon olive oil
2 medium carrots, peeled and cut into 1/4-inch pieces
1 medium onion, chopped
2 garlic cloves, crushed with garlic press
1 can (14 1/2 ounces) whole tomatoes in puree
1 can (14 1/2 ounces) vegetable broth (1 3/4 cups)
3/4 cup dry lentils, rinsed and picked through
1/2 teaspoon salt

1/2 teaspoon coarsely ground black pepper
1/4 teaspoon dried thyme
6 cups water
1 bunch Swiss chard (about 1 pound), trimmed and coarsely chopped
3/4 cup elbow macaroni (about 3 1/2 ounces)
1 cup fresh basil leaves, chopped
freshly grated Parmesan cheese (optional)

1. In nonstick 5- to 6-quart Dutch oven, heat oil over medium heat until hot. Add carrots, onion, and garlic and cook, stirring occasionally, until vegetables are tender and golden, about 10 minutes.

2. Add tomatoes with their puree, broth, lentils, salt, pepper, thyme, and water; heat to boiling, stirring to break up tomatoes with side of spoon. Reduce heat to low; cover and simmer until lentils are almost tender, about 20 minutes.

3. Stir in Swiss chard and macaroni; heat to boiling over medium-high heat. Reduce heat to medium; cook, uncovered, until macaroni is tender, about 10 minutes. Stir in basil. Serve with Parmesan, if you like.

Each serving without Parmesan: About 200 calories, 12g protein, 34g carbohydrate, 3g total fat (0g saturated), 0mg cholesterol, 810mg sodium.

Red Bean and Collard Gumbo

Gumbo is traditionally made with a variety of meats and shellfish, but you're not likely to be disappointed with this all-vegetable version.

Prep: 20 minutes   Cook: 30 minutes
Makes about 8 cups or 4 main-dish servings.

1/4 cup all-purpose flour
1 tablespoon olive oil
1 medium onion, thinly sliced
1 medium red pepper, cut into
  1/2-inch pieces
1 large stalk celery, thinly sliced
2 garlic cloves, crushed with
  garlic press
1/2 teaspoon salt
1/4 teaspoon ground red pepper
  (cayenne)

1/4 teaspoon dried thyme
1/4 teaspoon ground allspice
1 can (14 1/2 ounces) vegetable broth
  (1 3/4 cups)
3 cups water
1 bunch collard greens (about
  1 1/4 pounds), tough stems trimmed
  and leaves coarsely chopped
2 cans (15 to 19 ounces each) small
  red beans, rinsed and drained

1. In dry nonstick 5- to 6-quart saucepot, toast flour over medium heat, stirring frequently, until pale golden, about 5 minutes. Transfer flour to medium bowl; set aside.

2. In same saucepot, heat oil over medium-high heat until hot. Add onion, red pepper, and celery and cook, stirring occasionally, until vegetables are tender-crisp, about 10 minutes. Add garlic, salt, ground red pepper, thyme, and allspice and cook, stirring, 2 minutes.

3. Whisk broth into toasted flour until blended. Stir broth mixture and water into vegetables in saucepot; heat to boiling over medium-high heat. Add collard greens, stirring until wilted; stir in beans. Heat gumbo to boiling. Reduce heat to medium-low; cover and simmer until greens are tender, about 10 minutes.

Each serving: About 330 calories, 17g protein, 58g carbohydrate, 6g total fat (1g saturated), 0mg cholesterol, 1,190mg sodium.

Creamy Italian White Bean Soup

A perfect marriage of canned beans and fresh spinach, with a squeeze of fresh lemon juice for flavor.

PREP: 15 MINUTES   COOK: 40 MINUTES

MAKES ABOUT 6 CUPS OR 4 MAIN-DISH SERVINGS.

1 tablespoon vegetable oil
1 medium onion, finely chopped
1 medium stalk celery, finely chopped
1 garlic clove, minced
2 cans (15^1/$_2$ to 19 ounces each) white kidney beans (cannellini), rinsed and drained
1 can (14^1/$_2$ ounces) vegetable broth (1^3/$_4$ cups)

^{1}/$_4$ teaspoon coarsely ground black pepper
^{1}/$_8$ teaspoon dried thyme
2 cups water
1 bunch (10 to 12 ounces) spinach
1 tablespoon fresh lemon juice
freshly grated Parmesan cheese (optional)

1. In 3-quart saucepan, heat oil over medium heat until hot. Add onion and celery and cook, stirring occasionally, until tender, 5 to 8 minutes. Add garlic; cook, stirring, 30 seconds. Add beans, broth, pepper, thyme, and water; heat to boiling over high heat. Reduce heat to low; simmer, uncovered, 15 minutes.

2. Meanwhile, trim tough stems from spinach and discard; thinly slice leaves.

3. With slotted spoon, remove 2 cups bean-and-vegetable mixture from soup; set aside. Spoon half of remaining mixture into blender; cover, with center part of cover removed to let steam escape, and puree until smooth. Pour into large bowl. Repeat with remaining mixture.

4. Return soup to saucepan; stir in reserved beans and vegetables. Heat to boiling over high heat, stirring occasionally. Stir in spinach and cook until wilted, about 1 minute. Stir in lemon juice and remove from heat. Serve with Parmesan, if you like.

Each serving without Parmesan: About 295 calories, 18g protein, 46g carbo-hydrate, 5g total fat (1g saturated), 0mg cholesterol, 945mg sodium.

Creamy Italian White Bean Soup

Tomato and Rice Soup

Tomato and Rice Soup

Serve this old-fashioned comfort food with crusty bread and a tossed salad for a satisfying winter meal. If you can't find either Wehani (an aromatic, reddish-brown rice that splits slightly when cooked and has a chewy texture) or black Japonica (a dark rice that tastes like a cross between basmati and wild rice), you can use long-grain brown rice.

PREP: 20 MINUTES   COOK: 50 MINUTES

MAKES ABOUT 7 1/2 CUPS OR 4 MAIN-DISH SERVINGS.

1/2 cup Wehani, black Japonica, or long-grain brown rice
1 tablespoon butter or margarine
1 medium onion, finely chopped
1 medium stalk celery, finely chopped
1 medium carrot, peeled and chopped
1 garlic clove, crushed with garlic press
1/4 teaspoon dried thyme
1 can (28 ounces) plum tomatoes in juice

1 can (14 1/2 ounces) vegetable broth (1 3/4 cups)
1/2 teaspoon salt
1/4 teaspoon coarsely ground black pepper
1 bay leaf
1 cup water
1/2 cup loosely packed fresh parsley leaves, chopped

1. Prepare rice as label directs but do not add salt or butter; set rice aside.

2. Meanwhile, in 4-quart saucepan, melt butter over medium heat. Add onion, celery, and carrot and cook, stirring occasionally, until tender, about 10 minutes. Stir in garlic and thyme; cook 1 minute.

3. Add tomatoes with their juice, broth, salt, pepper, bay leaf, and water; heat to boiling over high heat, breaking up tomatoes with side of spoon. Reduce heat to medium-low and cook, covered, 30 minutes. Discard bay leaf.

4. Spoon one-third of mixture into blender; cover, with center part of cover removed to let steam escape, and puree until almost smooth. Pour into large bowl. Repeat with remaining mixture.

5. Return soup to saucepan; heat over high heat until hot. Remove saucepan from heat; add cooked rice and chopped parsley.

Each serving: About 190 calories, 6g protein, 32g carbohydrate, 6g total fat (4g saturated), 8mg cholesterol, 960mg sodium.

Mushroom and Brown Rice Soup

Instead of the more traditional barley, we prepare our version of this hearty soup with instant brown rice, reducing the cooking time.

PREP: 5 MINUTES: COOK: 25 MINUTES
MAKES ABOUT 8 CUPS OR 4 MAIN-DISH SERVINGS.

1 tablespoon olive oil
1 medium onion, finely chopped
1 package (10 ounces) sliced
  white mushrooms
1 package (4 ounces) assorted
  sliced wild mushrooms
1 cup shredded carrots
1 garlic clove, crushed with
  garlic press

1/2 teaspoon salt
1/4 teaspoon dried thyme
1/8 teaspoon ground black pepper
1 container (32 ounces) vegetable
  broth (4 cups)
3/4 cup instant brown rice
2 cups water

1. In 4-quart saucepan, heat oil over medium-high heat until hot. Add onion and cook, stirring occasionally, 5 minutes. Add mushrooms and carrots and cook, stirring occasionally, until golden and tender, 8 to 10 minutes. Add garlic, salt, thyme, and pepper and cook, stirring, 1 minute.
2. Add broth, rice, and water; cover and heat to boiling over high heat. Reduce heat to medium; cook, partially covered, until rice is tender, about 5 minutes.

Each serving: About 170 calories, 8g protein, 24g carbohydrate, 6g total fat (1g saturated), 0mg cholesterol, 1,260mg sodium.

Tomato, Escarole, and Tortellini Soup

For extra body and flavor, we've added a can of diced tomatoes with sweet onions to the Italian classic.

PREP: 10 MINUTES   COOK: 10 MINUTES
MAKES ABOUT 7 1/2 CUPS OR 4 MAIN-DISH SERVINGS.

8 ounces frozen or 1 package
(9 ounces) fresh tortellini or
mini ravioli
2 teaspoons olive oil
2 stalks celery, thinly sliced
1/2 medium head escarole, cut into
bite-size pieces (about 5 cups)

1 can (14 1/2 ounces) diced tomatoes
with sweet onions
1 can (14 1/2 ounces) vegetable broth
(1 3/4 cups)
1 cup water
1/4 cup freshly grated Romano
cheese

1. In 3-quart saucepan, cook pasta as label directs.
2. Meanwhile, in 4-quart saucepan, heat oil over medium heat. Add celery and cook, stirring occasionally, until tender-crisp, about 5 minutes. Stir in escarole, tomatoes, broth, and water. Cover and heat to boiling over high heat. Remove saucepan from heat.
3. Drain tortellini; gently stir into broth mixture. Divide soup evenly among 4 large bowls; sprinkle each serving with 1 tablespoon grated Romano.

Each serving: About 193 calories, 9g protein, 27g carbohydrate, 7g total fat (3g saturated), 13mg cholesterol, 1,149mg sodium.

Vegetable Soup with Bow Ties and Dill

Vegetable broth brimming with sautéed vegetables and tiny pasta bows is seasoned with a hint of lemon and lots of fresh dill—a perfect beginning to a light feast!

PREP: 25 MINUTES   COOK: 30 MINUTES
MAKES ABOUT 9 CUPS OR 4 MAIN-DISH SERVINGS.

1 lemon
1 tablespoon olive oil
1 large shallot, finely chopped
4 medium carrots, peeled and each
   cut lengthwise into quarters, then
   thinly sliced crosswise
2 medium stalks celery, thinly sliced

1 can (48 ounces) fat-free vegetable
   broth (6 cups)
1 cup water
1 package (10 ounces) frozen peas
3/4 cup small bow-tie pasta, cooked
3 tablespoons chopped fresh dill
1/8 teaspoon ground black pepper

1. From lemon, with vegetable peeler or small knife, remove 3" by 1" strip of peel; squeeze 1 tablespoon juice. Set aside.

2. In nonstick 5- to 6-quart saucepot, heat oil over medium-high heat until hot. Add shallot and cook, stirring frequently, until golden, about 2 minutes. Add carrots and celery and cook, stirring occasionally, until tender-crisp, about 5 minutes.

3. Add broth, lemon peel, and water; heat to boiling over medium-high heat. Reduce heat to low; cover and simmer until vegetables are tender, about 10 minutes.

4. Remove cover; stir in frozen peas and cook 1 minute longer. Stir in cooked pasta, dill, pepper, and lemon juice; heat through.

Each serving: About 240 calories, 10g protein, 34g carbohydrate, 4g total fat (2g saturated), 0mg cholesterol, 1540mg sodium.

Vegetable Soup with Bow Ties and Dill

Macaroni, Cabbage, and Bean Soup

Small pasta, such as macaroni or mini penne is perfect for this dish—
you can spoon up every last morsel.

PREP: 5 MINUTES   COOK: 15 MINUTES
MAKES 12 CUPS OR 6 MAIN-DISH SERVINGS.

1¹/₂ cups elbow macaroni or mini
   penne pasta
1 tablespoon olive oil
1 medium onion, cut in half and thinly
   sliced
¹/₂ small head Savoy cabbage (about
   1 pound), thinly sliced
2 garlic cloves, crushed with garlic
   press

¹/₄ teaspoon ground black pepper
3 cans (14¹/₂ ounces each)
   vegetable broth (5¹/₄ cups)
2 cans (15 to 19 ounces each) white
   kidney beans (cannellini), rinsed
   and drained
1¹/₂ cups water
freshly grated Parmesan cheese
   (optional)

1. In 4-quart saucepan, cook pasta as label directs.

2. Meanwhile, in 5- to 6-quart saucepot, heat oil over medium-high heat until hot. Add onion, cabbage, garlic, and pepper; cook, stirring often, until cabbage begins to wilt, 6 to 8 minutes. Stir in broth, beans, and water; heat to boiling.

3. Drain macaroni; stir into cabbage mixture and heat through. Serve with Parmesan, if you like.

Each serving: About 310 calories, 14g protein, 52g carbohydrate, 5g total fat (1g saturated), 0mg cholesterol, 1,170mg sodium.

Pasta e Fagioli

A fast-lane version of our favorite Italian bean soup.

PREP: 5 MINUTES COOK: 25 MINUTES
MAKES ABOUT 8 CUPS OR 4 MAIN-DISH SERVINGS.

1 tablespoon olive oil

1 small onion, sliced

1 large stalk celery, sliced

1 can (14 1/2 ounces) vegetable broth (1 3/4 cups)

2 cups water

1 can (15 to 19 ounces) white kidney beans (cannellini), rinsed and drained

1 can (14 1/2 ounces) diced tomatoes

2 garlic cloves, crushed with garlic press

1 teaspoon sugar

1/4 teaspoon salt

1/4 teaspoon ground black pepper

1/4 cup tubettini or ditalini pasta

1 package (10 ounces) frozen chopped spinach

1. In 5- to 6-quart Dutch oven, heat oil over medium heat until hot. Add onion and celery and cook, stirring occasionally, until vegetables are tender, about 10 minutes.

2. Meanwhile, in 2-quart saucepan, heat broth and water to boiling over high heat.

3. Add beans, tomatoes, garlic, sugar, salt, and pepper to onion mixture; heat to boiling over high heat. Add broth mixture and pasta; heat to boiling. Reduce heat to medium and cook 5 minutes. Add frozen spinach; cook, stirring frequently to separate spinach, 3 to 4 minutes longer.

Each serving: About 220 calories, 10g protein, 33g carbohydrate, 5g total fat (1g saturated), 0mg cholesterol, 1,265mg sodium.

French Onion Soup

Slowly cooked onions add great, caramelized flavor to this classic. If you double the recipe, be sure to cook the onions in two skillets.

PREP: 15 MINUTES   COOK/BAKE: 1 HOUR 50 MINUTES
MAKES 6 1/2 CUPS OR 4 MAIN-DISH SERVINGS.

3 tablespoons butter or margarine
7 medium onions (about 2 1/2
 pounds), each cut lengthwise in
 half and thinly sliced
1/4 teaspoon salt
4 cups water

1 can (14 1/2 ounces) vegetable broth
 (1 3/4 cups)
1/4 teaspoon dried thyme
4 slices (1/2 inch thick) French bread
4 ounces Gruyère or Swiss cheese,
 shredded (1 cup)

1. In 12-inch skillet, melt butter over medium heat. Add onions and salt and cook, stirring occasionally, until onions are very tender and begin to caramelize, about 45 minutes. Reduce heat to low; cook, stirring often, until onions are deep golden brown, about 15 minutes longer.
2. Transfer onions to 3-quart saucepan. Add 1/2 cup water to skillet; heat to boiling over high heat, stirring until browned bits are loosened from bottom of pan. Pour into saucepan with onions. Add broth, thyme, and remaining water; heat to boiling over high heat. Reduce heat to low; cover and simmer until onions are very tender, about 30 minutes.
3. Meanwhile, preheat oven to 450°F. Place bread slices on small cookie sheet; bake until lightly toasted, about 5 minutes.
4. Place four 2 1/2-cup oven-safe bowls in 15 1/2" by 10 1/2" jelly-roll pan. Spoon onion soup into bowls; top with toasted bread, pressing toast lightly into soup. Sprinkle toast with cheese. Bake until cheese melts and begins to brown, 12 to 15 minutes.

Each serving: About 375 calories, 15g protein, 38g carbohydrate, 23g total fat (11g saturated), 54mg cholesterol, 808mg sodium.

French Onion Soup

Vietnamese Noodle Soup

This Asian-style broth is brimming with delicate rice noodles, fresh snow peas, shiitake mushrooms, and pungent herbs.

Prep: 20 minutes   Cook: 25 minutes
Makes about 8 cups or 4 main-dish servings.

1 large lime
4 ounces dried flat rice noodles
  (about 1/4 inch wide)
2 cans (14 1/2 ounces each)
  vegetable broth
1 small bunch fresh basil
2 garlic cloves, crushed with side
  of chef's knife
1 piece (2 inches) peeled fresh
  ginger, thinly sliced

2 cups water
1/4 pound shiitake mushrooms, stems
  discarded and caps thinly sliced
4 ounces snow peas, strings removed
  and each pod cut diagonally in half
1 tablespoon soy sauce
1 cup loosely packed fresh cilantro
  leaves, chopped

1. From lime, with vegetable peeler, remove peel and reserve; squeeze 1 tablespoon juice.

2. In large bowl, pour enough *boiling water* over rice noodles to cover; let soak until softened, 7 to 10 minutes.

3. Meanwhile, in 3-quart saucepan, combine broth, basil, garlic, ginger, lime peel, and water; heat to boiling over high heat. Reduce heat to low; cover and simmer 10 minutes. Strain broth through sieve; discard solids and return broth to saucepan.

4. Drain noodles; rinse with cold running water and drain again. Stir mushrooms, snow peas, soy sauce, and noodles into broth mixture; heat to boiling over high heat. Reduce heat to low; cover and simmer 3 minutes. Stir in cilantro and lime juice just before serving.

Each serving: About 155 calories, 5g protein, 30g carbohydrate, 2g total fat (1g saturated), 0mg cholesterol, 1,120mg sodium.

Caldo Verde

This thick green soup is a Portuguese classic made with potatoes and very thinly sliced kale.

PREP: 15 MINUTES   COOK: 45 MINUTES
MAKES ABOUT 10 CUPS OR 5 MAIN-DISH SERVINGS.

2 tablespoons olive oil
1 large onion, diced
3 garlic cloves, minced
2 1/2 pounds all-purpose potatoes
    (about 8 medium), peeled and cut
    into 2-inch chunks
2 cans (14 1/2 ounces each)
    vegetable broth (3 1/2 cups)

3 cups water
1 teaspoon salt
1/4 teaspoon coarsely ground black
    pepper
1 pound kale, coarse stems and veins
    removed, very thinly sliced

1. In 5-quart Dutch oven, heat olive oil over medium heat. Add onion and garlic; cook until lightly browned, about 10 minutes.
2. Add potatoes, broth, water, salt, and pepper; heat to boiling over high heat. Reduce heat to low; cover and simmer until potatoes are fork-tender, about 20 minutes.
3. With potato masher, mash potatoes in broth until potatoes are lumpy. Stir in kale; simmer, uncovered, until tender, 5 to 8 minutes.

Each serving: About 250 calories, 8 g protein, 42 g carbohydrate, 7 g total fat (1 g saturated), 8 mg cholesterol, 925 mg sodium.

Sweet-Potato and Peanut Stew

Sweet-Potato and Peanut Stew

A tasty vegetarian dish with tomatoes, warm spices, and a touch of creamy peanut butter. Microwaving the sweet potatoes helps you finish in a flash.

PREP: 15 MINUTES. COOK: 15 MINUTES
MAKES ABOUT 8 CUPS OR 4 MAIN-DISH SERVINGS.

3 medium sweet potatoes (about 12 ounces each), well scrubbed and cut into 1½-inch pieces
1 tablespoon olive oil
2 garlic cloves, crushed with garlic press
1½ teaspoons ground cumin
½ teaspoon salt
¼ teaspoon ground cinnamon
⅛ teaspoon crushed red pepper
2 cans (15 to 19 ounces each) garbanzo beans, rinsed and drained
1 can (14½ ounces) vegetable broth (1¾ cups)
1 can (14½ ounces) diced tomatoes
¼ cup creamy peanut butter
½ cup loosely packed fresh cilantro leaves, chopped

1. Place potatoes in 2½-quart microwave-safe dish. Cover dish and microwave on High until fork-tender, about 8 minutes.

2. Meanwhile, in 5- to 6-quart saucepot, heat oil over medium-high heat until hot. Add garlic, cumin, salt, cinnamon, and crushed red pepper and cook, stirring, 30 seconds. Stir in beans, broth, tomatoes, and peanut butter until blended; heat to boiling and cook, stirring occasionally, 1 minute.

3. Reduce heat to medium-low; add sweet potatoes and simmer, stirring occasionally, 2 minutes. Stir in cilantro.

Each serving: About 585 calories, 22g protein, 92g carbohydrate, 16g total fat (2g saturated), 0mg cholesterol, 1,725mg sodium.

Curried Sweet-Potato and Lentil Soup

This thick and hearty soup is packed with spicy flavor. Get it going, then call a friend or spend some time with the kids while it simmers.

PREP: 15 MINUTES   COOK: 1 HOUR 15 MINUTES
MAKES ABOUT 14 CUPS OR 8 MAIN-DISH SERVINGS.

2 tablespoons butter or margarine
2 medium sweet potatoes (about
  12 ounces each), peeled and cut
  into 1/2-inch chunks
2 large stalks celery, cut into
  1/4-inch pieces
1 large onion (12 ounces), cut into
  1/4-inch pieces
1 garlic clove, minced
1 tablespoon curry powder
1 tablespoon grated, peeled
  fresh ginger

1 teaspoon ground cumin
1 teaspoon ground coriander
1 teaspoon salt
1/8 teaspoon ground red pepper
  (cayenne)
2 cans (14 1/2 ounces each)
  vegetable broth (3 1/2 cups)
1 package (16 ounces) dry lentils,
  rinsed and picked through
6 cups water
yogurt, toasted coconut, and lime
  wedges (optional)

1. In 6-quart Dutch oven, melt butter over medium heat. Add the sweet potatoes, celery, and onion and cook, stirring occasionally, until onion is tender, about 10 minutes. Add garlic, curry powder, ginger, cumin, coriander, salt, and ground red pepper; cook, stirring, 1 minute.

2. To vegetables in Dutch oven, add broth, lentils, and water; heat to boiling over high heat. Reduce heat to low; cover and simmer, stirring occasionally, until lentils are tender, 40 to 45 minutes. Serve with yogurt, toasted coconut, and lime wedges, if you like.

Each serving without yogurt, coconut, and lime: About 295 calories, 15g protein, 15g carbohydrate, 5g total fat (2g saturated), 8mg cholesterol, 646mg sodium.

Curried Sweet-Potato and Lentil Soup

Corn and Bean Chowder

This rich and creamy-looking soup—without a drop of cream—is easy to make, taking advantage of the convenience of canned beans and frozen corn.

PREP: 20 MINUTES   COOK: 35 MINUTES
MAKES ABOUT 12 CUPS OR 6 MAIN-DISH SERVINGS.

2 tablespoons olive oil
3 medium carrots, peeled and cut lengthwise in half, then crosswise into 1/4-inch-thick slices
1 large stalk celery, cut lengthwise in half, then crosswise into 1/4-inch-thick slices
1 large onion (12 ounces), chopped
1 medium red pepper, cut into 1/2-inch pieces
2 packages (10 ounces each) frozen whole-kernel corn

2 cups water
2 cans (15 to 16 ounces each) pink beans, rinsed and drained
2 cans (14 1/2 ounces each) vegetable broth (3 1/2 cups)
2 teaspoons sugar
1/2 teaspoon salt
1/4 teaspoon dried thyme
1/8 teaspoon ground red pepper (cayenne)

1. In 5- to 6-quart Dutch oven or saucepot, heat oil over medium heat until hot. Add carrots, celery, onion, and red pepper, and cook, stirring frequently, until vegetables are tender-crisp, about 10 minutes.
2. Meanwhile, in blender, combine 1 package frozen corn and water and puree until almost smooth.
3. To Dutch oven, add pureed corn mixture, remaining package frozen corn, beans, broth, sugar, salt, thyme, and ground red pepper; heat to boiling over high heat. Reduce heat to low; cover and simmer, stirring occasionally, 20 minutes.

Each serving: About 280 calories, 12g protein, 50g carbohydrate, 8g total fat (2g saturated), 0mg cholesterol, 1270mg sodium.

Tip
Cool soup slightly, and spoon into containers with tight-fitting lids. Refrigerate up to two days or freeze up to one month ahead. Reheat, without thawing, in Dutch oven, adding about two tablespoons water to pan to prevent scorching, or use the microwave.

Curried Vegetable Stew

A fast, fragrant skillet dish flavored with rich Indian spices, raisins, and tomatoes. Serve over rice or with pita bread and plain yogurt.

Prep: 30 minutes   Cook: 40 minutes
Makes about 10 cups or 5 main-dish servings.

1 tablespoon olive oil
1 medium onion, coarsely chopped
5 cups small cauliflower flowerets (about 1 small head cauliflower)
4 medium carrots, peeled and each cut lengthwise in half, then crosswise into 1/4-inch-thick slices
1 tablespoon minced, peeled fresh ginger
3 garlic cloves, crushed with garlic press
1 tablespoon curry powder

1 teaspoon ground cumin
3/4 teaspoon salt
1/8 to 1/4 teaspoon ground red pepper (cayenne)
2 cans (15 to 19 ounces each) garbanzo beans, rinsed and drained
1 can (14 1/2 ounces) diced tomatoes
1/4 cup golden raisins
1/2 cup water
1/2 cup loosely packed fresh cilantro leaves, chopped

1. In nonstick 12-inch skillet, heat oil over medium heat until hot. Add onion and cook, stirring occasionally, 5 minutes. Increase heat to medium-high; add cauliflower and carrots and cook, stirring occasionally, until vegetables are lightly browned, about 10 minutes. Add the ginger, garlic, curry powder, cumin, salt, and ground red pepper; cook, stirring, 1 minute.

2. Add garbanzo beans, tomatoes with their juice, raisins, and water; heat to boiling over high heat. Reduce heat to low; cover and simmer until vegetables are tender and sauce thickens slightly, 15 to 20 minutes. Stir in cilantro and serve.

Each serving: About 430 calories, 18g protein, 74g carbohydrate, 10g total fat (1g saturated), 0mg cholesterol, 1,430mg sodium.

Carrot and Apple Soup

Carrot and Apple Soup

If you own a hand blender, you can puree this winning combination of sweet carrots and apples right in the Dutch oven. We call for Golden Delicious apples for their consistently good flavor, but feel free to substitute other varieties.

PREP: 20 MINUTES   COOK: 35 MINUTES
MAKES ABOUT 10 CUPS OR 6 MAIN-DISH SERVINGS.

2 tablespoons butter or margarine
1 large onion (12 ounces), coarsely chopped
3 medium Golden Delicious apples
2 pounds carrots
2 cans (14 1/2 ounces each) vegetable broth
1 tablespoon sugar
1 teaspoon salt
1 teaspoon grated, peeled fresh ginger
2 cups water
half-and-half or heavy cream for garnish (optional)
fresh chives for garnish

1. In 5-quart Dutch oven, melt butter over medium heat. Add onion and cook, stirring occasionally, until tender and golden, about 12 minutes.
2. Meanwhile, peel apples and carrots. Cut each apple in half and remove core. Cut apples and carrots into 1 1/2-inch chunks.
3. Add apples, carrots, broth, sugar, salt, ginger, and water to onion; heat to boiling over high heat. Reduce heat to low; cover and simmer until carrots are very tender, about 20 minutes.
4. Remove Dutch oven from heat. Spoon one third of mixture into blender; cover, with center part of cover removed to let steam escape, and puree until very smooth.
5. Return soup to Dutch oven; heat through. Serve soup with a swirl of half-and-half, if you like. Garnish with fresh chives.

Each serving: About 173 calories, 3g protein, 30g carbohydrate, 7g total fat (3g saturated), 10mg cholesterol, 1,022mg sodium.

Broccoli and Cheddar Soup

For a satisfying meal, serve this rich soup with an artisinal multigrain bread and a crisp salad. Use a blender—not a food processor—for an extrasmooth texture.

PREP: 35 MINUTES   COOK: 25 MINUTES

MAKES ABOUT 8 CUPS OR 4 MAIN-DISH SERVINGS.

1 tablespoon olive oil
1 medium onion, chopped
1/4 cup all-purpose flour
1/2 teaspoon salt
1/4 teaspoon dried thyme
1/8 teaspoon ground nutmeg
coarsely ground black pepper
2 cups reduced-fat milk (2%)
1 can (141/2 ounces) vegetable broth
   (13/4 cups)

11/2 cups water
1 large bunch (11/2 pounds) broccoli,
   trimmed and cut into 1-inch pieces
   (including stems)
11/2 cups shredded sharp Cheddar
   cheese (6 ounces)
coarsely ground black pepper

1. In 4-quart saucepan, heat oil over medium heat until hot. Add onion and cook, stirring occasionally, until golden, about 10 minutes. Stir in flour, salt, thyme, nutmeg, and 1/4 teaspoon pepper; cook, stirring frequently, 2 minutes.

2. Gradually stir in milk, broth, and water. Add broccoli and heat to boiling over high heat. Reduce heat to low; cover and simmer until broccoli is tender, about 10 minutes.

3. Spoon one-third of mixture into blender; cover, with center part of cover removed to let steam escape, and puree until very smooth. Pour into large bowl. Repeat with remaining batches.

4. Return the soup to saucepan; heat to boiling over high heat, stirring occasionally. Remove saucepan from heat; stir in cheese until melted and smooth. Sprinkle each serving with coarsely ground black pepper.

Each serving: About 362 calories, 24g protein, 26g carbohydrate, 22g total fat (12g saturated), 52mg cholesterol, 934mg sodium.

Chunky Vegetable Chowder

Using an assortment of favorite fall vegetables in this hearty soup makes it a tasty and healthful comfort food.

PREP: 20 MINUTES   COOK: 30 MINUTES
MAKES ABOUT 13 CUPS OR 6 MAIN-DISH SERVINGS.

2 tablespoons olive oil
1 jumbo onion (1 pound), cut into
   1/4-inch pieces
12 ounces red potatoes, unpeeled
   and cut into 1/2-inch pieces
3 medium carrots, peeled and cut
   into 1/4-inch pieces
2 medium parsnips (about 8 ounces),
   peeled and cut into 1/4-inch pieces
2 medium stalks celery, cut into
   1/4-inch pieces

2 garlic cloves, crushed with
   garlic press
1 can (141/2 ounces) vegetable broth
   (13/4 cups)
3/4 teaspoon salt
1/4 teaspoon dried thyme
41/2 cups water
1 package (10 ounces) frozen
   Fordhook lima beans
12 ounces escarole or Swiss chard,
   trimmed and coarsely chopped

1. In nonstick 5- to 6-quart saucepot or Dutch oven, heat oil over medium-high heat until very hot. Add onion, potatoes, carrots, parsnips, celery, and garlic and cook, stirring occasionally, until vegetables are lightly browned, 15 minutes.

2. Add broth, salt, thyme, and water; heat to boiling over medium-high heat. Stir in lima beans and escarole; heat to boiling. Reduce heat to low; cover and simmer until vegetables are tender, about 10 minutes.

Each serving: About 220 calories, 7g protein, 39g carbohydrate, 5g total fat (1g saturated), 0mg cholesterol, 675mg sodium.

Chilled Buttermilk-Vegetable Soup

The refreshing, cool flavors of summer vegetables make this chunky soup a delightful first course.

Prep: 20 minutes plus chilling
Makes about 10 cups or 6 main-dish servings.

2 limes
1½ quarts buttermilk (6 cups)
3 medium tomatoes (about 1 pound), seeded and cut into ¼-inch pieces
1 English (seedless) cucumber, unpeeled and cut into ¼-inch pieces
1 ripe avocado, cut into ¼-inch pieces

1 cup loosely packed fresh cilantro leaves, chopped
1 teaspoon salt
¼ teaspoon coarsely ground black pepper
cilantro sprigs for garnish

1. From limes, grate 1 teaspoon peel and squeeze 3 tablespoons juice.
2. In large bowl, combine lime peel and juice, buttermilk, tomatoes, cucumber, avocado, cilantro, salt, and pepper; stir until blended. Cover and refrigerate at least 2 hours or up to one day. Garnish each serving with a cilantro sprig.

Each serving: About 175 calories, 10g protein, 18g carbohydrate, 6g total fat (2g saturated), 8mg cholesterol, 632mg sodium.

Green Pea and Lettuce Soup

Fresh chives add color as well as flavor to this simplified lowfat version of the delicate French classic.

PREP: 5 MINUTES   COOK: 15 MINUTES
MAKES ABOUT 6 CUPS OR 4 MAIN-DISH SERVINGS.

2 teaspoons butter or margarine
1 medium onion, finely chopped
1 can (14 1/2 ounces) vegetable broth
  (1 3/4 cups)
1 package (10 ounces) frozen peas
1 head Boston lettuce (about
  10 ounces), coarsely chopped

3/4 teaspoon salt
1/8 teaspoon ground black pepper
1/8 teaspoon dried thyme
1 cup water
1/2 cup fat-free (skim) milk
1 tablespoon fresh lemon juice
fresh chives for garnish

1. In 4-quart saucepan, melt butter over medium heat. Add onion and cook, stirring occasionally, until tender, about 5 minutes. Stir in broth, frozen peas, lettuce, salt, pepper, thyme, and water; heat to boiling over high heat. Reduce heat to low; simmer 5 minutes. Stir in milk.

2. Spoon half of pea mixture into blender; cover, with center part of cover removed to let steam escape, and puree until smooth. Pour soup into large bowl. Repeat with remaining mixture.

3. Return soup to same saucepan; heat through. Stir in lemon juice and remove from heat. Transfer soup to serving bowl; garnish with chives.

Each serving: About 120 calories, 8g protein, 17g carbohydrate, 4g total fat (2g saturated), 6mg cholesterol, 829mg sodium.

Mushroom-Barley Miso Soup

Simmer shiitake mushrooms and barley in a miso broth. Never boil miso; its delicate flavor and nutrients will be destroyed by high heat.

PREP: 20 MINUTES   COOK: 1 HOUR
MAKES ABOUT 10 CUPS OR 6 MAIN-DISH SERVINGS.

1 package (1 ounce) dried shiitake
   mushrooms
1 tablespoon olive oil
3 medium carrots, peeled and cut
   into 1/4-inch pieces
1 medium onion, chopped
2 garlic cloves, minced
1 tablespoon grated, peeled fresh ginger

1/2 cup pearl barley
1/2 teaspoon salt
1/4 teaspoon coarsely ground
   black pepper
11/2 pounds bok choy, trimmed and
   chopped
6 tablespoons dark red miso
1 tablespoon brown sugar

1. In 2-quart saucepan, heat *4 cups water* to boiling over high heat. Remove saucepan from heat; add dried shiitake mushrooms and let stand until softened, about 15 minutes. With slotted spoon, remove mushrooms. Rinse to remove any grit; drain on paper towels. Cut stems from mushrooms and discard; thinly slice caps. Strain soaking liquid through sieve lined with paper towels into 4-cup glass measuring cup. Add enough *water* to liquid in cup to equal 4 cups and set aside.

2. In nonstick 5-quart Dutch oven, heat oil over medium heat until hot. Add carrots, onion, and mushrooms and cook, stirring occasionally, until vegetables are tender, about 15 minutes. Add garlic and ginger and cook 1 minute longer.

3. Add barley, salt, pepper, reserved mushroom liquid, and an additional *4 cups water;* heat to boiling over medium-high heat. Reduce heat to low; cover and simmer until barley is tender, about 40 minutes.

4. Add bok choy; heat to boiling over medium-high heat. Reduce heat to low and simmer, uncovered, until bok choy is tender-crisp and wilted, 5 to 7 minutes, stirring occasionally.

5. With ladle, transfer 1/2 cup broth from soup to small bowl. Add miso and brown sugar to broth and stir until smooth paste forms.

6. Remove Dutch oven from heat; stir in miso mixture.

Each serving: About 170 calories, 7g protein, 29g carbohydrate, 4g total fat (0g saturated), 0mg cholesterol, 985mg sodium.

Thai Coconut Soup

For a more authentic—fiery—flavor, increase the ground red pepper to taste or, if available, add a small red Szechuan pepper or two (be sure to remove the peppers before serving).

PREP: 14 MINUTES   COOK: 6 MINUTES
MAKES ABOUT 9 CUPS OR 4 MAIN-DISH SERVINGS.

2 small carrots, peeled and each cut crosswise in half
1/2 medium red pepper
1 can (14 ounces) light unsweetened coconut milk (not cream of coconut), well stirred
2 garlic cloves, crushed with garlic press
1 piece (2 inches) peeled fresh ginger, cut into 4 pieces
1/2 teaspoon ground coriander
1/2 teaspoon ground cumin

1/4 teaspoon ground red pepper (cayenne)
12 ounces firm tofu, cut into 1-inch cubes
2 cans (14 1/2 ounces each) vegetable broth (3 1/2 cups)
1 tablespoon Asian fish sauce (nuoc nam, see Tip below)
1 tablespoon fresh lime juice
1 cup water
2 green onions, trimmed and sliced
1/2 cup chopped fresh cilantro leaves

1. With vegetable peeler, remove lengthwise strips from carrots and edge of red pepper; set aside.
2. In 5-quart Dutch oven, heat 1/2 cup coconut milk to boiling over medium heat. Add garlic, ginger, coriander, cumin, and ground red pepper and cook, stirring, 1 minute.
3. Increase heat to medium-high. Stir in tofu, broth, carrot strips, pepper strips, fish sauce, lime juice, water, and remaining coconut milk; heat just to simmering. Discard ginger. Just before serving, stir in green onions and cilantro.

Each serving: About 210 calories, 11g protein, 14g carbohydrate, 17g total fat (6g saturated), 0mg cholesterol, 1,060mg sodium.

Tip
Asian fish sauce (nuoc nam or nam pla) is available in the specialty sections of some supermarkets and in Asian groceries.

Hot and Sour Soup

We streamlined seasonings to help get this popular Asian soup on the table in record time—without sacrificing the great taste.

PREP: 10 MINUTES: COOK: 20 MINUTES
MAKES ABOUT 8 CUPS OR 4 MAIN-DISH SERVINGS.

1 tablespoon vegetable oil

4 ounces shiitake mushrooms, stems removed and caps thinly sliced

3 tablespoons reduced-sodium soy sauce

1 package (15 to 16 ounces) extrafirm tofu, drained, patted dry, and cut into 1-inch cubes

2 tablespoons cornstarch

1 container (32 ounces) vegetable broth (4 cups)

3 tablespoons seasoned rice vinegar

2 tablespoons grated, peeled fresh ginger

1 tablespoon Worcestershire sauce

1/2 teaspoon Asian sesame oil

1/4 teaspoon ground red pepper (cayenne)

2 large eggs, beaten

2 green onions, trimmed and sliced

1. In nonstick 5-quart saucepot, heat vegetable oil over medium-high heat until hot. Add mushrooms, soy sauce, and tofu and cook, gently stirring often, until liquid has evaporated, about 5 minutes.

2. In cup, with fork, blend cornstarch and *1/4 cup water* until smooth; set aside. Add broth and *3/4 cup water* to tofu mixture; heat to boiling. Stir in cornstarch mixture and boil, stirring, 30 seconds. Reduce heat to medium-low; add vinegar, ginger, Worcestershire, sesame oil, and pepper and simmer 5 minutes.

3. Remove saucepot from heat. In a thin, steady stream, slowly pour beaten eggs into soup around side of saucepot. Carefully stir soup once in circular motion to separate egg into strands. Sprinkle with green onions.

Each serving: About 280 calories, 18g protein, 17g carbohydrate, 15g total fat (3g saturated), 106mg cholesterol, 1,790mg sodium.

Tip

To brown, tofu should be dry. Wrap in paper towels and set it on a plate. Cover with a second plate; place a heavy can on top and let drain fifteen minutes. Discard towels.

Harvest Mexican Soup

This soup is full of savory ingredients, including corn, avocado, and lime; a jalapeño chile adds a burst of heat.

PREP: 25 MINUTES   COOK: 30 MINUTES
MAKES ABOUT 9 1/2 CUPS OR 4 MAIN-DISH SERVINGS.

4 teaspoons olive oil
1 jumbo onion (1 pound), cut into
  1/4-inch pieces
2 medium carrots, peeled and cut
  into 1/4-inch pieces
2 garlic cloves, crushed with
  garlic press
1 jalapeño chile, seeded and minced
3 limes
12 ounces red potatoes, unpeeled
  and cut into 1/4-inch pieces

1 can (14 1/2 ounces) vegetable broth
  (1 3/4 cups)
1/2 teaspoon salt
4 cups water
2 cups corn kernels cut from cobs
  (3 to 4 ears)
1 cup loosely packed fresh cilantro
  leaves, chopped
1 avocado, cut into 1/4-inch pieces
plain tortilla chips, coarsely broken
  (optional)

1. In nonstick 5- to 6-quart saucepot or Dutch oven, heat oil over medium-high heat until hot. Add onion, carrots, garlic, and jalapeño, and cook, stirring occasionally, until vegetables are golden, 15 minutes.
2. Meanwhile, from limes, grate 1/2 teaspoon peel and squeeze 1/3 cup juice; set aside.
3. Add potatoes, broth, salt, and water to saucepot; heat to boiling over medium-high heat. Reduce heat to low; cover and simmer 5 minutes. Add corn; cover and simmer until potatoes are tender, about 5 minutes.
4. Stir in cilantro, lime peel, and lime juice. Ladle soup into 4 bowls; top with avocado and sprinkle with tortilla chips, if you like.

Each serving: About 350 calories, 8g protein, 58g carbohydrate, 14g total fat (2g saturated), 0mg cholesterol, 945mg sodium.

LUNCH AND BRUNCH

French Potato Pancake

Whether you spend your days at work, at school, or at home, weekday lunch has become a meal to be consumed quickly, between getting to the next meeting, class, or activity. Finding time to have a relaxing, well-balanced, wholesome lunch can be difficult.

But weekends are another story. Life slows to a more manageable pace and, while there may be chores to do or places to go, we can sleep late and get out of the weekday routine. Many of us use the extra time to start the day off with a leisurely brunch—that weekend meal that combines the best of both breakfast and lunch, and that carries us right through to dinner.

Of course, when you think brunch, the first thing that comes to mind are eggs, one of nature's most nutrient-rich and versatile foods. Not only are eggs an inexpensive protein source, they provide a tasty base for using up leftover veggies, cheese, and herbs. And for added convenience, most egg recipes can be doubled to accommodate a crowd.

In the pages that follow, you'll find eggs baked in pies, tarts, frittatas, and quiches; scrambled and in omelets; poached in a spicy tomato sauce, and on top of a mixture of salsa and black beans for Tex-Mex fans. And for those weekends when you're having house guests, nothing beats a make-ahead Spinach Strata, a savory, custardy Italian-style baked bread pudding.

There are lots of non-egg dishes to choose from, too. They can be as simple as substantial sandwiches—Fresh Mozzarella and Tomato with piquant green salsa on crisp country bread and Greek Salad in Pitas are only two examples. For big appetites, the gyro-style Portobello "Cheese Steaks" with sautéed sweet peppers and onions fills the bill. Delight kids and grown-ups alike when you serve the colorful, layered French Potato Pancake, with its choice of three ethnic-style fillings.

In addition to being healthful and palate-pleasing, the recipes in this chapter yield leftovers that are ideal for packing in a brown bag or lunch box. Now there's no excuse for not eating healthy all week long.

Falafel Sandwiches

Serve these small, flat bean patties in pita pockets with lettuce, tomatoes, cucumbers, red onion, and tangy plain low-fat yogurt.

PREP: 10 MINUTES   COOK: 8 MINUTES PER BATCH
MAKES 4 SANDWICHES.

4 green onions, cut into 1-inch pieces
2 garlic cloves, each cut in half
1/2 cup packed fresh flat-leaf parsley
2 teaspoons dried mint
1 can (15 to 19 ounces) garbanzo beans, rinsed and drained
1/2 cup plain dried bread crumbs
1 teaspoon ground coriander
1 teaspoon ground cumin
1 teaspoon baking powder

1/2 teaspoon salt
1/4 teaspoon ground red pepper (cayenne)
1/4 teaspoon ground allspice
olive oil cooking spray
4 (6- to 7-inch) pitas
accompaniments: sliced romaine lettuce, sliced tomatoes, sliced cucumber, sliced red onion, plain low-fat yogurt

1. In food processor, with knife blade attached, finely chop green onions, garlic, parsley, and mint. Add garbanzo beans, bread crumbs, coriander, cumin, baking powder, salt, ground red pepper, and allspice; blend until coarse puree forms.

2. Shape bean mixture, by scant 1/2 cups, into eight 3-inch round patties and place on sheet of waxed paper. Spray both sides of patties with olive oil spray.

3. Heat nonstick 10-inch skillet over medium-high heat until hot. Add half of patties and cook, turning once, until dark golden brown, about 8 minutes. Transfer the falafel patties to paper towels to drain. Repeat with remaining patties.

4. Cut off top third of each pita to form pocket. Place 2 warm patties in each pita. Serve with choice of accompaniments.

Each sandwich without accompaniments: About 365 calories, 14g protein, 68g carbohydrate, 5g total fat (1g saturated), 0mg cholesterol, 1,015mg sodium.

Greek Salad Pitas

Hummus—the Middle Eastern spread made with mashed garbanzo beans—is fast work in a food processor or blender.

PREP: 20 MINUTES

MAKES 4 SANDWICHES.

1 can (15 to 19 ounces) garbanzo
  beans, rinsed and drained
1/4 cup plain lowfat yogurt
2 tablespoons olive oil
2 tablespoons fresh lemon juice
1/2 teaspoon salt
1/4 teaspoon coarsely ground
  black pepper
1/4 teaspoon ground cumin
1 garlic clove, peeled
4 (6- to 7-inch) whole-wheat pitas

3 cups sliced romaine lettuce
2 medium tomatoes, cut into
  1/4-inch pieces
1 medium cucumber, peeled and
  thinly sliced
2 ounces feta cheese, crumbled
  (about 1/2 cup)
2 tablespoons chopped fresh
  mint leaves
fresh mint leaves for garnish

1. In food processor, with knife blade attached, or in blender, combine beans, yogurt, oil, lemon juice, salt, pepper, cumin, and garlic and puree until smooth.

2. Cut off top third of each pita to form pocket. Use half of the bean mixture to spread inside pockets.

3. Combine lettuce, tomatoes, cucumber, feta, and chopped mint; use to fill pockets. Top with remaining bean mixture and mint leaves.

Each sandwich: About 440 calories, 17g protein, 66g carbohydrate, 15g total fat (4g saturated), 13mg cholesterol, 1,105mg sodium.

Greek Salad Pitas

Huevos Rancheros

This traditional Mexican dish is a quick and easy way to liven up breakfast or brunch.

PREP: 5 MINUTES COOK: 7 MINUTES
MAKES 4 MAIN-DISH SERVINGS.

1 can (15 to 19 ounces) black beans, rinsed and drained
1¼ cups mild or medium-hot salsa (about 11 ounces)
¼ cup water
4 large eggs

3 ounces shredded Mexican cheese blend (¾ cup)
chopped fresh cilantro or parsley leaves for garnish
warm flour tortillas (optional)

1. In 10-inch skillet, mix black beans, salsa, and water; heat to boiling over high heat, stirring frequently.

2. Break eggs, one at a time, into custard cup and slip into skillet on top of bean mixture. Reduce heat to medium-low; cover and simmer until whites are completely set and yolks begin to thicken, about 5 minutes, or until eggs are cooked to desired firmness.

3. To serve, sprinkle bean mixture and eggs with shredded cheese and garnish with chopped cilantro. Serve with warm tortillas, if you like.

Each serving without tortillas: About 250 calories, 17g protein, 23g carbohydrate, 12g total fat (6g saturated), 231mg cholesterol, 1,110mg sodium.

Eggs in Spicy Tomato Sauce

This classic Italian dish pairs an easy homemade tomato sauce with eggs poached right in the sauce. A delicious one-skillet dish to add to your quick-cook repertoire.

PREP: 15 MINUTES   COOK: 30 MINUTES
MAKES 4 MAIN-DISH SERVINGS.

1 loaf (8 ounces) Italian bread
1 tablespoon olive oil
1 jumbo onion (1 pound), cut into
  1/4-inch pieces
2 medium carrots, peeled and cut
  into 1/4-inch pieces
1 stalk celery, cut into 1/4-inch pieces
2 garlic cloves, crushed with
  garlic press

1 can (28 ounces) whole tomatoes
1/2 teaspoon salt
1/4 teaspoon crushed red pepper
1 tablespoon butter or margarine
8 large eggs
1/4 cup loosely packed fresh
  basil leaves, chopped

1. Preheat oven to 350°F. Cut bread diagonally into 1-inch-thick slices. Place bread slices on cookie sheet and bake until lightly toasted, about 5 minutes. Set aside.

2. In nonstick 12-inch skillet, heat oil over medium-high heat until hot. Add onion, carrots, celery, and garlic and cook, stirring occasionally, until vegetables are lightly browned, 12 to 15 minutes.

3. Stir in tomatoes with their juice, salt, and crushed red pepper, breaking up tomatoes with side of spoon; heat to boiling over medium-high heat. Reduce heat to low; simmer, stirring occasionally, 5 minutes. Stir in butter.

4. Break 1 egg into custard cup. With back of spoon, make small well in sauce and slip egg into well. Repeat with remaining eggs. Heat sauce to boiling over medium-high heat. Reduce heat to medium-low; cover and simmer until egg whites are set and yolks begin to thicken, 7 to 10 minutes, or until eggs are cooked to desired firmness.

5. To serve, place 1 bread slice in each of 4 large soup bowls. Spoon 2 eggs and some tomato mixture over each slice; sprinkle with basil. Serve with remaining bread.

Each serving: About 455 calories, 21g protein, 52g carbohydrate, 20g total fat (6g saturated), 433mg cholesterol, 1,091mg sodium.

Cream Cheese and Chive Scrambled Eggs

Cream Cheese and Chive Scrambled Eggs

Serve this versatile dish for a formal brunch or for a late-night family supper. A salad on the side rounds out the meal.

PREP: 5 MINUTES   COOK: 5 MINUTES

MAKES 4 MAIN-DISH SERVINGS.

1 bag (5 ounces) baby mixed salad greens
1 tablespoon olive oil
2 teaspoons red wine vinegar
pinch plus 1/2 teaspoon salt
8 large eggs
2 tablespoons chopped fresh chives
1/4 teaspoon coarsely ground black pepper

1/4 cup water
2 teaspoons butter or margarine
4 ounces (half 8-ounce package) Neufchâtel or light cream cheese, cut into 1/2-inch pieces
4 slices multigrain bread, toasted and each cut diagonally in half

1. In medium bowl, toss greens with oil, vinegar, and pinch salt; set aside.
2. In large bowl, with wire whisk, beat eggs, chives, pepper, remaining 1/2 teaspoon salt, and water until blended.
3. In nonstick 10-inch skillet, melt butter over medium-high heat; add egg mixture. With heat-safe rubber spatula, gently push egg mixture as it begins to set to form soft curds. When eggs are partially cooked, top with Neufchâtel and continue cooking, stirring occasionally, until eggs have thickened and no visible liquid egg remains.
4. To serve, divide greens among 4 dinner plates. Place 2 toast halves on each plate; spoon eggs over toast.

Each serving: About 340 calories, 18g protein, 15g carbohydrate, 24g total fat (9g saturated), 451mg cholesterol, 716mg sodium.

Leek and Goat Cheese Quiche

Meltingly tender sweet leeks and tangy goat cheese are delicious partners in this rich tart.

PREP: 30 MINUTES PLUS CHILLING AND COOLING   BAKE: 60 MINUTES
MAKES 8 MAIN-DISH SERVINGS.

Pastry for 11-inch tart (recipe follows)

FILLING

1 pound leeks (about 3 medium)
2 tablespoons butter or margarine
1/2 teaspoon salt
1/2 cup water
3 large eggs

1 log (31/2 to 4 ounces) mild goat cheese such as Montrachet
1/8 teaspoon ground black pepper
11/2 cups half-and-half or light cream

1. Prepare Pastry for 11-inch Tart as recipe directs.

2. On lightly floured surface, with floured rolling pin, roll dough into 14-inch round. Ease dough into 11" by 1" round tart pan with removable bottom. Fold overhang in and press dough against side of pan so it extends 1/8 inch above rim. With fork, prick dough at 1-inch intervals. Refrigerate 30 minutes or freeze 10 minutes. Preheat oven to 425°F.

3. Line tart shell with foil; fill with pie weights or dry beans. Bake 10 minutes. Remove foil with weights; bake until lightly golden, about 10 minutes longer. (If pastry puffs up during baking, gently press down with back of spoon.) Cool in pan on wire rack 20 minutes. Turn oven control to 350°F.

4. While tart shell bakes and cools, prepare filling: Cut off roots and trim dark green tops from leeks. Cut each leek lengthwise in half, then crosswise into 1/2-inch-thick slices. Rinse leeks in large bowl of cold water, swishing to remove sand; transfer to colander to drain, leaving sand in bottom of bowl.

5. In 12-inch skillet, melt butter over medium heat. Add leeks, 1/4 teaspoon salt, and water; cook, uncovered, until leeks are tender and all liquid has evaporated, about 10 minutes, stirring occasionally. Remove skillet from heat.

6. In medium bowl, with wire whisk, beat eggs, goat cheese, pepper, and remaining 1/4 teaspoon salt until well blended. Stir in half-and-half.

7. Place tart pan on foil-lined cookie sheet to catch any overflow. Sprinkle leeks over bottom of tart shell; pour egg mixture over leeks. Bake until knife inserted in center comes out clean, 35 to 40 minutes. Cool on wire rack 10 minutes. Just before serving, remove side of pan. Serve hot or at room temperature.

Each serving: About 410 calories, 10g protein, 26g carbohydrate, 31g total fat (17g saturated), 149mg cholesterol, 551mg sodium.

Pastry for 11-inch Tart

PREP: 10 MINUTES PLUS CHILLING
MAKES ONE 11-INCH TART SHELL.

1¹/₂ cups all-purpose flour	2 tablespoons vegetable shortening
¹/₂ teaspoon salt	3 to 4 tablespoons ice water
¹/₂ cup cold butter or margarine (1 stick), cut into pieces	

1. In large bowl, mix flour and salt. With pastry blender or two knives used scissor-fashion, cut in butter and shortening until mixture resembles coarse crumbs.

2. Sprinkle in ice water, 1 tablespoon at a time, mixing lightly with fork after each addition, until dough is just moist enough to hold together. Shape dough into disk; wrap disk in plastic wrap. Refrigerate 30 minutes or up to overnight. (If chilled overnight, let stand 30 minutes at room temperature before rolling.)

Each ¹/₈ pastry: About 222 calories, 3g protein, 20g carbohydrate, 15g total fat (8g saturated), 32mg cholesterol, 263mg sodium.

Asparagus Quiche

We made the delicate custard filling with half-and-half instead of heavy cream to save fat and calories—but it still tastes rich.

PREP: 45 MINUTES PLUS CHILLING AND COOLING
BAKE: 40 TO 45 MINUTES
MAKES 8 MAIN-DISH SERVINGS.

1¼ cups all-purpose flour
¾ teaspoon salt
4 tablespoons butter or margarine
2 tablespoons shortening
4 tablespoons ice water
1 pound asparagus, trimmed and cut into ¾-inch pieces

4 large eggs
2 cups half-and-half or light cream
⅛ teaspoon ground black pepper
pinch ground nutmeg
4 ounces Gruyère or Swiss Cheese, coarsely shredded (1 cup)

1. In medium bowl, mix flour and ¼ teaspoon salt. With pastry blender or two knives used scissor-fashion, cut in butter and shortening until mixture resembles coarse crumbs. Sprinkle in ice water, 1 tablespoon at a time, mixing lightly with fork after each addition, until dough is just moist enough to hold together. Shape dough into disk; wrap in plastic wrap. Refrigerate 30 minutes or up to overnight. (If chilled overnight, let stand 30 minutes at room temperature before rolling.)

2. Meanwhile, in 2-quart saucepan, heat *4 cups water* to boiling over high heat. Add asparagus and cook until tender, 6 to 8 minutes. Drain asparagus and rinse under cold water. Drain and set aside.

3. Preheat oven to 425°F. On lightly floured surface, with floured rolling pin, roll dough into 11-inch round. Gently ease dough into 9-inch pie plate. Fold overhang in and press dough against side of pan so it extends ⅛ inch above rim. Make decorative edge. With fork, prick dough at 1-inch intervals.

4. Line pie shell with foil; fill with pie weights or dry beans. Bake 15 minutes. Remove foil with weights; bake until golden, about 10 minutes longer. (If crust puffs up during baking, gently press it down with back of spoon.) Turn oven control to 350°F.

5. Meanwhile, in medium bowl, with wire whisk, beat eggs, half-and-half, pepper, nutmeg, and remaining ½ teaspoon salt until well blended.
6. Place pie plate on foil-lined cookie sheet to catch any overflow. Sprinkle asparagus and cheese over bottom of crust; pour egg mixture over asparagus and cheese. Bake until knife inserted in center comes out clean, 40 to 45 minutes. Serve hot or at room temperature.

Each serving: About 325 calories, 12g protein, 19g carbohydrate, 25g total fat (12g saturated), 157mg cholesterol, 362mg sodium.

Asparagus Omelet

If you don't have pale yellow, nutty-flavored Gruyère cheese, substitute the same amount of shredded Swiss or Jarlsberg, or a few shavings of fresh Parmesan.

PREP: 10 MINUTES   COOK: 5 MINUTES
MAKES 4 MAIN-DISH SERVINGS.

FILLING
1 pound asparagus, trimmed
1/8 teaspoon coarsely ground black pepper
4 ounces Gruyère cheese, shredded (1 cup)

OMELETS
8 large eggs (see Tip below)
1/2 teaspoon salt
1/2 cup cold water
4 teaspoons butter or margarine

1. Prepare filling: In deep 12-inch skillet, heat *1 inch water* to boiling over high heat. Add asparagus; heat to boiling. Reduce heat and simmer, uncovered, just until tender, about 5 minutes. Drain and rinse with cold running water. Drain. Sprinkle pepper over cheese.

2. To make omelets: In medium bowl, with wire whisk, beat eggs, salt, and cold water. For each omelet, in nonstick 8-inch skillet, melt 1 teaspoon butter over medium-high heat. Pour in 1/2 cup egg mixture; cook, gently lifting edge of eggs with heat-safe rubber spatula and tilting pan to allow uncooked eggs to run underneath, until eggs are set, about 1 minute. Sprinkle one-fourth of cheese mixture over half of omelet; top with one-fourth of asparagus spears. Fold unfilled half over filling and slide onto warm plate. Repeat with remaining butter, egg mixture, and filling. If desired, keep omelets warm in 200°F oven until all are cooked.

Each omelet: About 310 calories, 23g protein, 3g carbohydrate, 25g total fat (11g saturated), 467mg cholesterol, 528mg sodium.

Tip
For lighter omelets, substitute 4 large eggs and 8 large egg whites for the whole eggs.

Asparagus Omelet

Greens and Ricotta Pie

It's like a quiche without the crust! Swiss chard and green onion make up this savory dish—an easy entrée for lunch or brunch.

PREP: 30 MINUTES   BAKE: 40 MINUTES
MAKES 6 MAIN-DISH SERVINGS.

1 large head Swiss chard (about 1 3/4 pounds)
1 tablespoon olive oil
1 bunch green onions, cut into 1/4-inch-thick pieces
1/2 teaspoon salt
1/4 teaspoon coarsely ground black pepper

4 large eggs
1 container (15 ounces) part-skim ricotta cheese
3/4 cup low-fat milk (1%)
1/2 cup freshly grated Parmesan cheese
2 tablespoons cornstarch

1. Preheat oven to 350°F. Grease 9 1/2-inch deep-dish glass pie plate.

2. Trim off 2 inches from Swiss-chard stems; discard ends. Separate stems from leaves; thinly slice stems and coarsely chop leaves.

3. In nonstick 12-inch skillet, heat oil over medium-high heat until hot. Add sliced stems and cook, stirring frequently, until tender and lightly browned, about 4 minutes. Add green onions, salt, and pepper and cook 1 minute. Gradually add chopped leaves and cook, stirring, until leaves have wilted and excess moisture has evaporated, about 5 minutes.

4. In large bowl, with wire whisk, beat eggs, ricotta, milk, Parmesan, and cornstarch. Stir in Swiss-chard mixture.

5. Place prepared pie plate on foil-lined cookie sheet to catch any overflow. Pour mixture into pie plate. Bake pie until knife inserted 2 inches from center comes out clean, about 40 minutes.

Each serving: About 255 calories, 19g protein, 14g carbohydrate, 14g total fat (7g saturated), 172mg cholesterol, 680mg sodium.

Frittata Sandwiches with Peppers and Onions

This hot sandwich can be wrapped in foil and carried along to serve later at a backyard picnic or concert in the park.

PREP: 30 MINUTES   BAKE: 10 MINUTES
MAKES 4 SANDWICHES.

2 tablespoons olive oil
2 medium onions, each cut in half
  and thinly sliced
4 Italian frying peppers (about
  2 ounces each), thinly sliced
1/2 teaspoon salt
6 large eggs

3/4 cup freshly grated Parmesan
  cheese
1/4 cup chopped fresh parsley
1/4 teaspoon ground black pepper
1 round or square (8-inch) focaccia
  bread, cut horizontally in half

1. In 12-inch skillet, heat 1 tablespoon oil over medium heat. Add onions and cook, stirring frequently, until tender, about 8 minutes. Add peppers; sprinkle with 1/4 teaspoon salt and cook until peppers are tender, about 12 minutes longer. Keep warm.

2. Meanwhile, preheat oven to 375°F. In large bowl, with wire whisk beat eggs, Parmesan, parsley, black pepper, and remaining 1/4 teaspoon salt until blended.

3. In oven-safe nonstick 10-inch skillet (if skillet is not oven-safe, wrap handle with double layer of foil), heat remaining 1 tablespoon olive oil over medium heat. Pour in egg mixture and cook, without stirring, until egg mixture begins to set around the edge, 3 to 4 minutes.

4. Place skillet in oven; bake until frittata is just set and knife inserted in center comes out clean, about 10 minutes longer. Slide frittata onto plate.

5. Place frittata on bottom of focaccia; top with onion mixture. Replace top of focaccia. To serve, cut into 4 wedges.

Each sandwich: About 535 calories, 29g protein, 49g carbohydrate, 26g total fat (7g saturated), 341mg cholesterol, 1,225mg sodium.

Spring Onion, Spinach, and Pecorino Frittata

For a less assertive flavor, substitute Parmigiano-Reggiano for the Pecorino Romano or use a combination of the two for a more complex flavor.

PREP: 30 MINUTES   BAKE: 10 MINUTES
MAKES 4 MAIN-DISH SERVINGS.

2 spring onions with tops (about 12 ounces), or 1 large (12 ounces) sweet onion
2 teaspoons olive oil
1 bag (5 to 6 ounces) baby spinach
8 large eggs
1/4 cup freshly grated Pecorino Romano cheese
1/4 cup water
1/2 teaspoon salt
1/4 teaspoon coarsely ground black pepper

1. Preheat oven to 425°F. Trim tough green leaves from top of spring onions. Cut stems crosswise into 1/4-inch-thick slices. Cut each onion bulb in half and thinly slice.

2. In oven-safe nonstick 12-inch skillet (if skillet is not oven-safe, wrap handle with double layer of foil), heat oil over medium heat until hot. Add sliced onions and stems and cook, stirring occasionally, until soft and golden brown, about 10 minutes. Stir in spinach and cook, stirring constantly, just until wilted, about 1 minute. Spread onion mixture evenly in skillet; remove skillet from heat.

3. In medium bowl with wire whisk, beat eggs, Pecorino Romano, water, salt, and pepper until blended. Carefully pour egg mixture over onion mixture; do not stir. Return skillet to medium-high heat and cook until egg mixture begins to set around the edge, 2 to 3 minutes.

4. Place skillet in oven; bake until frittata is set, 8 to 10 minutes. Slide frittata onto cutting board. Cut into wedges to serve.

Each serving: About 215 calories, 16g protein, 7g carbohydrate, 14g total fat (4g saturated), 430mg cholesterol, 530mg sodium.

Asparagus and Green Onion Frittata

Everyone loves a skillet omelet, especially when it's filled with bits of cream cheese and sautéed vegetables.

PREP: 25 MINUTES   BAKE: 10 MINUTES
MAKES 4 MAIN-DISH SERVINGS.

8 large eggs
1/2 cup whole milk
1/8 teaspoon ground black pepper
3/4 teaspoon salt
12 ounces asparagus, trimmed

1 tablespoon butter or margarine
1 bunch green onions, chopped
2 ounces light cream cheese (Neufchâtel)

1. Preheat oven to 375°F. In medium bowl, with wire whisk, beat eggs, milk, pepper, and 1/2 teaspoon salt until blended; set aside. If using thin asparagus, cut each stalk crosswise in half; if using medium asparagus, cut stalks into 1-inch pieces.

2. In oven-safe nonstick 10-inch skillet (if skillet is not oven-safe, wrap handle with double layer of foil), melt butter over medium heat. Add the asparagus and the remaining 1/4 teaspoon salt and cook, stirring often, 4 minutes for thin stalks or 6 minutes for medium-size stalks. Stir in green onions and cook, stirring occasionally, until vegetables are tender, 2 to 3 minutes longer.

3. Reduce heat to medium-low. Pour egg mixture over vegetables; drop scant teaspoonfuls of cream cheese over egg mixture. Cook, without stirring, until egg mixture begins to set around edge, 3 to 4 minutes. Place skillet in oven and bake until frittata is set and knife inserted in center comes out clean, 10 to 12 minutes. Cut into wedges to serve.

Each serving: About 250 calories, 17g protein, 6g carbohydrate, 19g total fat (7g saturated), 448mg cholesterol, 671mg sodium.

Spinach and Jack Cheese Bread Pudding

A delicious departure from quiche, this savory bread pudding is easier to prepare and very satisfying.

PREP: 5 MINUTES BAKE: 25 MINUTES
MAKES 6 MAIN-DISH SERVINGS.

6 large eggs
2 cups low-fat milk (1%)
1/4 teaspoon dried thyme
1/4 teaspoon salt
1/4 teaspoon coarsely ground
   black pepper
pinch ground nutmeg

1 package (10 ounces) frozen
   chopped spinach, thawed and
   squeezed dry
1 cup shredded Monterey Jack
   cheese (4 ounces)
8 slices firm white bread, cut into
   3/4-inch pieces

1. Preheat oven to 375°F. In large bowl, with wire whisk, beat eggs, milk, thyme, salt, pepper, and nutmeg until blended. With rubber spatula, stir in spinach, Monterey Jack, and bread.

2. Pour mixture into lightly greased 13" by 9" ceramic or glass baking dish. Bake bread pudding until browned and puffed, and knife inserted in center comes out clean, 20 to 25 minutes.

3. Remove bread pudding from oven; let stand 5 minutes before serving.

Each serving: About 280 calories, 17g protein, 22g carbohydrate, 13g total fat (6g saturated), 233mg cholesterol, 545mg sodium.

Spinach and Jack Cheese Bread Pudding

Spinach Strata

Spinach Strata

You can assemble this a day ahead, then pop it in the oven—right from the refrigerator—just one hour before serving.

PREP: 15 MINUTES PLUS CHILLING   BAKE: 1 HOUR
MAKES 6 MAIN-DISH SERVINGS.

8 slices firm white bread
4 ounces mozzarella cheese, shredded (1 cup)
1 package (10 ounces) frozen chopped spinach, thawed and squeezed dry
1 tablespoon butter or margarine, softened

2 cups milk
6 large eggs
$1/2$ cup loosely packed fresh basil leaves, chopped
$1/2$ teaspoon salt
$1/4$ teaspoon ground black pepper

1. Grease 8" by 8" glass baking dish. Place 4 bread slices in dish; top with $1/2$ cup cheese, all spinach, then remaining cheese. Spread butter on 1 side of each remaining bread slice; place in dish, buttered side up.

2. In medium bowl, with wire whisk, beat milk, eggs, basil, salt, and pepper until blended. Slowly pour egg mixture over bread slices. Prick bread with fork and press slices down to absorb egg mixture. Cover baking dish with plastic wrap and refrigerate at least 30 minutes or overnight.

3. Preheat oven to 350°F. Remove cover from baking dish; bake strata until knife inserted in center comes out clean, about 1 hour. Remove from oven and let stand 5 minutes before serving.

Each serving: About 290 calories, 17g protein, 22g carbohydrate, 16g total fat (7g saturated), 245mg cholesterol, 569mg sodium.

Savory Rice and Ricotta Tart

An irresistible combination of rice and creamy ricotta cheese baked with spinach in a golden crust.

Prep: 30 minutes   Bake: 1 hour
Makes 8 main-dish servings.

Pastry for 11-inch Tart (page 71)

RICE FILLING

$1/2$ cup long-grain white rice
$3/4$ teaspoon salt
1 cup water
1 tablespoon butter or margarine
1 medium onion, finely chopped
1 package (10 ounces) frozen chopped spinach, thawed and squeezed dry

$1/4$ teaspoon coarsely ground black pepper
$1/8$ teaspoon ground nutmeg
1 container (15 ounces) part-skim ricotta cheese
$1/2$ cup low-fat milk (1%)
3 large eggs
$3/4$ cup freshly grated Parmesan cheese

1. Prepare Pastry for 11-inch Tart as recipe directs.

2. Preheat oven to 425°F. On lightly floured surface, with floured rolling pin, roll dough into 14-inch round. Ease dough into 11" by 1" round tart pan with removable bottom. Fold overhang in and press dough against side of pan so it extends $1/8$ inch above rim. With fork, prick dough at 1-inch intervals.

3. Line tart shell with foil and fill with pie weights or dry beans. Bake tart shell 20 minutes; remove foil with weights, and bake until golden, about 10 minutes longer. (If pastry puffs up during baking, gently press down with back of spoon.) Turn oven control to 350°F.

4. While tart shell is baking, prepare filling: In 1-quart saucepan, heat rice, $1/4$ teaspoon salt, and water to boiling over high heat. Reduce heat to low; cover and simmer until rice is tender and liquid has been absorbed, 15 to 18 minutes.

5. While rice is cooking, in 2-quart saucepan, melt butter over medium heat. Add onion and cook until tender, about 8 minutes. Stir in spinach, pepper, nutmeg, and remaining $1/2$ teaspoon salt; remove from heat.

6. In large bowl, with wire whisk, mix ricotta, milk, eggs, and ½ cup Parmesan until well blended. Stir in cooked rice and spinach mixture.

7. Spoon rice mixture into warm tart shell; spread evenly. Sprinkle remaining ¼ cup Parmesan over filling. Bake until set, about 30 minutes. (To brown top after baking, turn oven control to broil. Place tart on rack in broiling pan. Place pan in broiler at closest position to heat source; broil 3 to 5 minutes.) Remove side of pan and serve tart warm.

Each serving: About 415 calories, 17g protein, 34g carbohydrate, 29g total fat (14g saturated), 139mg cholesterol, 690mg sodium.

Summer Squash and Potato Frittata with Sage

It takes just a few teaspoons of minced sage to jazz up a humble egg entrée—we love it for brunch or supper.

PREP: 50 MINUTES   BAKE: 15 MINUTES
MAKES 6 MAIN-DISH SERVINGS.

1 large all-purpose potato (8 ounces), peeled and cut into 1/2-inch pieces
1 1/2 teaspoons salt
2 tablespoons butter or margarine
1 medium red onion, thinly sliced
2 garlic cloves, minced
1 small yellow summer squash (about 4 ounces), cut into 2" by 1/4" strips

1 small zucchini (about 4 ounces), cut into 2" by 1/4" strips
2 teaspoons minced fresh sage leaves
1/4 teaspoon coarsely ground black pepper
8 large eggs
2 teaspoons balsamic vinegar

1. Preheat oven to 350°F. In 2-quart saucepan, combine potato, 1/2 teaspoon salt, and *enough water to cover*; heat to boiling over high heat. Reduce heat to low; cover and simmer until tender, about 10 minutes. Drain.

2. Meanwhile, in oven-safe nonstick 10-inch skillet (if skillet is not oven-safe, wrap handle with double layer of foil), melt butter over medium heat. Add onion and cook, stirring occasionally, until very soft, about 12 minutes.

3. Stir in the garlic; cook 1 minute. Add cooked potato, yellow squash, zucchini, sage, pepper, and remaining 1 teaspoon salt and cook, stirring occasionally, until zucchini is tender and liquid has evaporated, about 12 minutes.

4. In medium bowl, with wire whisk, beat eggs and vinegar. Pour egg mixture over vegetables in skillet and cook, covered, over medium heat until mixture begins to set around edge, about 3 minutes.

5. Remove cover and place skillet in oven; bake until frittata is set, about 15 minutes. Cut into wedges to serve.

Each serving: About 180 calories, 10g protein, 11g carbohydrate, 13g total fat (5g saturated), 294mg cholesterol, 528mg sodium.

Puffy Cheese Grits

Grits are a breakfast tradition throughout the South, where it is served with a pat of melting butter or a spoonful of redeye gravy (made by adding coffee to the skillet a ham steak was fried in). Southerners have perfected grits by baking them with plenty of cheese until they're hot and puffy, making this a dish enjoyed by all—whether you grew up eating grits or not.

PREP: 20 MINUTES   BAKE: 45 MINUTES
MAKES 8 MAIN-DISH SERVINGS.

3 1/2 cups milk
2 cups water
2 tablespoons butter or margarine
1 teaspoon salt
1 1/4 cups quick hominy grits

8 ounces Cheddar cheese, shredded (2 cups)
5 large eggs
1 teaspoon hot pepper sauce
1/4 teaspoon ground black pepper

1. Preheat oven to 325°F. Lightly grease shallow 2 1/2-quart casserole.

2. In 3-quart saucepan, combine 1 1/2 cups milk, water, butter, and salt; heat to boiling over medium-high heat. With wire whisk, gradually stir in grits, constantly beating to prevent lumps. Reduce heat; cover and cook, stirring occasionally with a wooden spoon, 5 minutes (grits will be very stiff). Remove from heat and stir in Cheddar.

3. In large bowl, with wire whisk, beat eggs, remaining 2 cups milk, hot pepper sauce, and black pepper until blended. Gradually stir grits mixture into egg mixture until well combined.

4. Pour grits mixture into prepared casserole. Bake until knife inserted in center comes out clean, about 45 minutes.

Each serving: About 338 calories, 16g protein, 24g carbohydrate, 21g total fat (12g saturated), 193mg cholesterol, 595mg sodium.

Portobello Burgers

Portobello Burgers

Marinate the "burgers" in a broth mixture accented with thyme before grilling, and serve on buns with a lemon and green-onion mayonnaise.

PREP: 15 MINUTES PLUS MARINATING   GRILL: 20 MINUTES
MAKES 4 SANDWICHES.

1/4 cup vegetable broth
2 tablespoons olive oil
2 teaspoons balsamic vinegar
1 teaspoon chopped fresh
    thyme leaves
1/4 teaspoon salt
1/4 teaspoon coarsely ground
    black pepper
4 medium (about 4 ounces each)
    portobello mushrooms, stems
    removed

1 lemon
1/3 cup mayonnaise
1 small green onion, trimmed
    and minced
4 large (about 4-inch) buns
1 bunch arugula, trimmed

1. In glass baking dish just large enough to hold mushrooms in a single layer, mix broth, oil, vinegar, thyme, 1/8 teaspoon salt, and 1/8 teaspoon pepper. Add mushrooms, turning to coat. Let stand, turning occasionally, 30 minutes.

2. Prepare grill.

3. Meanwhile, from lemon, grate 1/2 teaspoon peel and squeeze 1/2 teaspoon juice. In small bowl, stir lemon peel and juice, mayonnaise, green onion, and remaining 1/8 teaspoon salt and 1/8 teaspoon pepper.

4. Place mushrooms on hot grill rack over medium heat and grill, turning occasionally and brushing with remaining marinade, until mushrooms are browned and cooked through, 8 to 10 minutes per side.

5. Cut each bun horizontally in half. Spread cut sides of buns with mayonnaise mixture; top with arugula leaves. Place warm mushrooms on bottom halves of buns; replace top half of buns to serve.

Each sandwich: About 355 calories, 6g protein, 30g carbohydrate, 25g total fat (4g saturated), 7mg cholesterol, 585mg sodium.

Portobello "Cheese Steaks"

Portobello "Cheese Steaks"

A hearty hand-held meal wrapped in pita and served gyro style.

PREP: 15 MINUTES   COOK: 20 MINUTES
MAKES 4 SANDWICHES.

2 medium portobello mushrooms
 (about 4 ounces each), stems
 removed
2 tablespoons olive oil
2 medium yellow peppers, thinly
 sliced
1 jumbo sweet onion (1 pound) such
 as Vidalia or Walla Walla, thinly
 sliced

1/2 teaspoon salt
1/4 teaspoon coarsely ground black
 pepper
2 tablespoons water
1 tablespoon balsamic vinegar
4 (7-inch) pocketless pitas
8 ounces part-skim mozzarella
 cheese, shredded (2 cups)

1. Preheat oven to 400°F. Heat nonstick 12-inch skillet over medium-high heat until hot. Brush both sides of mushrooms using 1 tablespoon oil. Add mushrooms to skillet and cook until tender and lightly browned, about 5 minutes on each side. Transfer mushrooms to cutting board and cut into 1/4-inch-thick slices; set aside.

2. In same skillet, heat remaining 1 tablespoon oil over medium heat until hot. Add yellow peppers, onion, salt, black pepper, and water; cook, stirring frequently, until the vegetables are tender and golden, about 15 minutes. Stir in vinegar; remove skillet from heat. Gently stir in sliced portobellos.

3. Meanwhile, place pitas on large cookie sheet; sprinkle with mozzarella cheese. Heat pitas until cheese has melted, about 5 minutes.

4. Roll each pita into a cone; tightly wrap bottom half of each with kitchen parchment or foil to help hold its shape and prevent leakage. Fill pita cones with warm mushroom mixture.

Each sandwich: About 460 calories, 24g protein, 52g carbohydrate, 18g total fat (7g saturated), 41mg cholesterol, 1,060mg sodium.

Potato Pancakes and Carrot-Parsley Salad

There are as many recipes for potato pancakes as there are families that make them. To save time, we use a bag of preshredded hash-brown potatoes, which are found in the refrigerator case of your supermarket. To round out the meal, prepare the simple but tasty carrot salad.

PREP: 10 MINUTES   COOK: 15 MINUTES
MAKES 4 MAIN-DISH SERVINGS.

POTATO PANCAKES
1/2 **cup vegetable oil for frying**
1 **teaspoon salt**
1/8 **teaspoon ground black pepper**
2 **large eggs**
1 **(20-ounce) bag refrigerated shredded hash-brown potatoes (4 cups)**
2 **green onions, trimmed and thinly sliced**

CARROT-PARSLEY SALAD
1 **tablespoon fresh lemon juice**
1 **tablespoon extravirgin olive oil**
1/4 **teaspoon salt**
1 **package (10 ounces) shredded carrots**
1 **cup packed fresh parsley leaves**
applesauce and sour cream

1. Preheat oven to 250°F. Line the cookie sheet with paper towels. In 12-inch skillet, heat oil over medium–high heat until very hot.

2. Meanwhile, prepare pancakes: In medium bowl, mix salt, pepper, and eggs; stir in potatoes and green onions. Drop mixture by scant 1/2 cups into hot oil to make 4 pancakes. With back of spoon, flatten each pancake into 4-inch oval. Cook until golden on both sides, 5 to 7 minutes. With slotted spatula, transfer pancakes to prepared cookie sheet to drain; keep warm in oven. Repeat with remaining mixture.

3. While pancakes cook, prepare salad: In small bowl or cup, with fork, stir lemon juice, oil, and salt until blended.

4. In salad bowl, combine carrots and parsley. Pour dressing over salad and toss to coat evenly.

5. Serve pancakes with applesauce and sour cream, and a side of carrot-parsley salad.

Each serving: About 395 calories, 8g protein, 41g carbohydrate, 23g total fat (3g saturated), 106mg cholesterol, 890mg sodium.

Potato Pancakes and Carrot-Parsley Salad

French Potato Pancake

We've taken the classic Swiss shredded-potato pancake and come up with a choice of fillings designed to please everyone. This versatile recipe can serve as a main dish or an accompaniment.

PREP: 25 MINUTES   BAKE: 25 MINUTES
MAKES 4 MAIN-DISH SERVINGS.

PEPPER FILLING

2 teaspoons olive oil
1 medium red pepper, cut into
  1/4-inch pieces
3 1/2 to 4 ounces plain goat cheese, crumbled

POTATO PANCAKE

2 1/4 pounds baking potatoes
  (about 4 medium)
1/2 teaspoon salt
1/2 teaspoon coarsely ground
  black pepper
2 tablespoons olive oil

1. Prepare filling: In oven-safe nonstick 10-inch skillet (if skillet is not oven-safe, wrap handle with double layer of foil), heat oil over medium heat until hot. Add red pepper and cook, stirring occasionally, until tender and lightly browned, 10 to 12 minutes. Transfer pepper to small bowl; set aside. Wipe skillet with paper towel.

2. Meanwhile, prepare potato pancake: Preheat oven to 400°F. Peel and coarsely shred potatoes; pat dry with paper towels. In large bowl, toss potatoes with salt and black pepper.

3. In same skillet, heat 1 tablespoon oil over medium heat. Working quickly, add half of potatoes, gently patting with rubber spatula to cover bottom of skillet. Leaving 1-inch border, top potatoes with red pepper and goat cheese. Cover filling with remaining potatoes, gently patting to edge of skillet. Cook, gently shaking skillet occasionally to keep pancake from sticking, until browned, 10 minutes.

4. Carefully invert pancake onto large, flat plate. Add remaining 1 tablespoon oil to skillet, then slide pancake back into skillet. Cook, gently shaking skillet occasionally, 10 minutes longer.

5. Place skillet, uncovered, in oven and bake until potatoes are tender throughout, 20 to 25 minutes.

Each serving: About 340 calories, 10g protein, 36g carbohydrate, 18g total fat (8g saturated), 22mg cholesterol, 550mg sodium.

French Potato Pancake

Swiss Potato Pancake: Prepare French Potato Pancake as above, but in step 1, instead of preparing pepper filling, heat *1 tablespoon oil* in skillet over medium heat until hot. Add *1 large onion (12 ounces)*, cut into ¼-inch pieces, and cook, stirring occasionally, until tender and golden brown, about 15 minutes. Transfer onion to small bowl. Complete recipe as in steps 2 through 5, substituting caramelized onion and *1 cup shredded Gruyère cheese (4 ounces)* for red pepper and goat cheese.

Each serving: About 370 calories, 12g protein, 38g carbohydrate, 20g total fat (6g saturated), 30mg cholesterol, 380mg sodium.

Mexican Potato Pancake: Prepare French Potato Pancake as above, but in step 1, instead of preparing pepper filling, in small bowl, stir *1 cup canned black beans*, rinsed, drained, and mashed; *1 tablespoon water, 1 teaspoon fresh lime juice*, and *½ teaspoon ground cumin* until well mixed. (If bean mixture is too stiff to spread, stir in *1 or 2 teaspoons water*.) Complete recipe as in steps 2 through 5, substituting black-bean mixture and *1 cup shredded Monterey Jack cheese (4 ounces)* for red pepper and goat cheese.

Each serving: About 360 calories, 12g protein, 42g carbohydrate, 16g total fat (6g saturated), 30mg cholesterol, 530mg sodium.

Old-Time Tomato Sandwiches

We love these as is or with a few sprigs of watercress tucked inside.

PREP: 15 MINUTES
MAKES 4 SANDWICHES.

1 lemon
1/3 cup mayonnaise
1/4 teaspoon ground coriander
1/4 teaspoon salt
1/4 teaspoon coarsely ground black
  pepper

1 large round or oval loaf (1 pound)
  sourdough or other crusty bread
3 large ripe tomatoes, thickly sliced

1. From lemon, grate 1/2 teaspoon peel and squeeze 1 teaspoon juice. In small bowl, with fork, stir lemon peel and juice, mayonnaise, coriander, salt, and pepper until blended.
2. Cut eight 1/2-inch-thick slices from center of bread loaf. Reserve ends for another use. Toast bread if desired.
3. Spread 1 side of each bread slice with mayonnaise mixture. Top each of 4 bread slices, mayonnaise side up, with tomato slices; top with re-maining bread slices, mayonnaise side down. Cut each sandwich in half to serve.

Each sandwich: About 300 calories, 6g protein, 35g carbohydrate, 18g total fat (3g saturated), 7mg cholesterol, 540mg sodium.

Old-Time Tomato Sandwiches

Fresh Mozzarella and Tomato Sandwiches

The essence of summer, with garden tomatoes and our versatile Italian herb sauce, which makes a terrific sandwich spread.

PREP: 15 MINUTES
MAKES 4 SANDWICHES.

1/2 cup Salsa Verde (below)
8 slices (1/2 inch thick) Tuscan bread
2 ripe medium tomatoes, each cut
   into 4 slices

8 ounces fresh mozzarella cheese,
   cut into 8 slices

Spread about 1 tablespoon Salsa Verde on 1 side of each bread slice. On each of 4 bread slices, sauce side up, place 2 tomato slices and 2 mozzarella slices. Top with remaining bread slices, sauce side down. Cut each sandwich in half to serve.

Each sandwich: About 455 calories, 17g protein, 38g carbohydrate, 26g total fat (9g saturated), 44mg cholesterol, 690mg sodium.

Salsa Verde

1 garlic clove, cut in half
1/4 teaspoon salt
2 cups packed fresh flat-leaf parsley
   leaves (about 3 bunches)
1/3 cup olive oil

3 tablespoons capers, drained
3 tablespoons fresh lemon juice
1 teaspoon Dijon mustard
1/8 teaspoon ground black pepper

In food processor with knife blade attached, or in blender, combine garlic, salt, parsley, oil, capers, lemon juice, mustard, and pepper and puree until almost smooth. If not using right away, cover and refrigerate up to 3 days. Makes about 3/4 cup.

Each tablespoon: About 60 calories, 0g protein, 1g carbohydrate, 6g total fat (1g saturated), 0mg cholesterol, 140mg sodium.

Vegetarian Souvlaki

No one will miss the meat in these yummy sandwiches. Make the filling by cutting up your favorite veggie burgers.

PREP: 15 MINUTES   COOK: 20 MINUTES
MAKES 4 MAIN-DISH SERVINGS.

1 tablespoon olive oil
1 large onion (12 ounces), cut in half and thinly sliced
4 frozen vegetarian soy burgers (10- to 12-ounce package), cut into 1-inch pieces
1/2 teaspoon salt
1/4 teaspoon ground black pepper
8 ounces plain nonfat yogurt

8 ounces English (seedless) cucumber, cut into 1/4-inch pieces
1 teaspoon dried mint
1 small garlic clove, crushed with garlic press
4 (6- to 7-inch) pitas, warmed
1 medium tomato, cut into 1/2-inch pieces
1 ounce feta cheese, crumbled

1. In nonstick 12-inch skillet, heat oil over medium heat until hot. Add onion and cook, stirring occasionally, until tender and golden, 12 to 15 minutes. Add burgers, 1/4 teaspoon salt, and pepper and cook until heated through, about 5 minutes.

2. Meanwhile, in medium bowl, stir yogurt, cucumber, mint, garlic, and remaining 1/4 teaspoon salt until blended. Add burger mixture and toss gently to combine.

3. Cut 1-inch slice from each pita to form pocket. Spoon one-fourth burger mixture into each pita. Sprinkle with tomato and feta.

Each sandwich: About 390 calories, 24g protein, 45g carbohydrate, 13g total fat (3g saturated), 9mg cholesterol, 945mg sodium.

MAIN-DISH SALADS

Flatbread with Salad

S alads can be an extremely versatile part of vegetarian menus year round. They can be served chilled in the summer and warm during the colder months. Although we usually think of salads as a combination of vegetables tossed with greens, they can take many forms. Pasta, grains, beans and legumes, eggs, potatoes, even bread can serve as the foundation of a salad. Then just add fresh seasonal fruits or vegetables and other vegetarian staples, and maybe some whole-grain bread as an accompaniment, and you have a hearty, nutritious meal.

The art of salad making lies in the composition and combination of ingredients. Essential to any salad is the freshest, finest-quality produce available. The best salads contrast and balance textures, colors, and flavors. Crunchy and soft ingredients, tangy flavors with slightly sweet or mild ones, and bright colors combined with muted ones create salads that are pleasing to both the eyes and the taste buds.

The recipes we selected for this chapter are some of our favorites. You'll recognize variations on familiar standbys, such as Egg Salad Deluxe, with sautéed onions, mushrooms, and celery. Because salads are part of cuisines all over the world, we've included many with an international flair. Rice Salad with Black Beans, featuring corn and watercress, is a zesty south-of-the-border meal in a bowl. Szechuan Peanut-Noodle Salad with linguini and snow peas is as satisfying hot as it is chilled. Or try Fattoush, a refreshing Lebanese salad of tomatoes, cucumber, scallions, and romaine, napped with a lemon-herb dressing, to which pieces of toasted pita are added to absorb the luscious flavors.

Include a basket of whole-grain breads or crackers and perhaps another vegetarian dish on the table as accompaniments for an especially hearty meal. If you want to add extra protein in the form of nuts or seeds, toast them briefly for best flavor. For protein, you can also add full-flavored cheeses like feta, Parmesan, or gorgonzola; crumbled hard-cooked eggs; or other tasty add-ins that complement the ingredients. If there are meat lovers at the table, put out a plate of sliced grilled chicken or beef and let them help themselves. Salads are a great way to indulge your culinary creativity as you plan wholesome vegetarian meals for your family.

Black Bean and Avocado Salad with Cilantro Dressing

A satisfying combination of summer veggies, romaine lettuce, and black beans tossed with a creamy cilantro-lime dressing.

PREP: 30 MINUTES

MAKES ABOUT 16 CUPS OR 4 MAIN-DISH SERVINGS.

CILANTRO DRESSING

2 limes
1/4 cup light mayonnaise
1/2 cup packed fresh cilantro leaves
2 tablespoons reduced-fat sour cream
1/2 teaspoon ground cumin
1/4 teaspoon sugar
1/8 teaspoon salt
1/8 teaspoon coarsely ground
    black pepper

SALAD

1 small head romaine lettuce (about
    1 pound), cut into 3/4-inch pieces
    (about 8 cups)
2 medium tomatoes, cut into 1/2-inch
    pieces
2 Kirby cucumbers (about 4 ounces
    each), unpeeled, each cut
    lengthwise into quarters, then
    crosswise into 1/4-inch-thick pieces
1 ripe avocado, cut into 1/2-inch
    pieces
1 can (15 to 19 ounces) black beans,
    rinsed and drained

1. Prepare dressing: From limes, grate 1/2 teaspoon peel and squeeze 3 tablespoons juice. In blender, combine lime peel and juice, mayonnaise, cilantro, sour cream, cumin, sugar, salt, and pepper and puree, occasionally scraping down sides of blender, until smooth. Cover and refrigerate if not using right away. Makes about 1/2 cup.

2. Prepare salad: In large serving bowl, combine romaine, tomatoes, cucumbers, avocado, and beans. Add dressing and toss until evenly coated.

Each serving: About 230 calories, 9g protein, 34g carbohydrate, 10g total fat (2g saturated), 3mg cholesterol, 520mg sodium.

Rice Salad with Black Beans

A satisfying meal in one, packed with the zesty flavors of citrus, salsa, and cilantro.

PREP: 10 MINUTES   COOK: 20 MINUTES

MAKES ABOUT 7 CUPS OR 4 MAIN-DISH SERVINGS.

3/4 cup regular long-grain rice

2 large limes

2 cans (15 to 19 ounces) black beans, rinsed and drained

1 bunch watercress, tough stems removed

1/2 cup bottled salsa

1 cup corn kernels cut from cobs (2 medium ears)

1/4 cup packed fresh cilantro leaves, chopped

1 tablespoon olive oil

1/2 teaspoon salt

1/4 teaspoon coarsely ground black pepper

1. Prepare rice as label directs. Meanwhile, from limes, grate 1/2 teaspoon peel and squeeze 3 tablespoons juice.

2. In large bowl, mix cooked rice, lime peel and juice, black beans, watercress, salsa, corn, cilantro, oil, salt, and pepper; toss well. Cover and refrigerate if not serving right away.

Each serving: About 405 calories, 24g protein, 81g carbohydrate, 6g total fat (1g saturated), 0mg cholesterol, 1,125mg sodium.

Wheat-Berry Salad with Spinach

Wheat berries, the whole unprocessed kernels, can be found in health food stores. They have a nutlike sweetness and a satisfyingly chewy texture.

PREP: 15 MINUTES PLUS SOAKING   COOK: 1 HOUR 15 MINUTES
MAKES 4 MAIN-DISH SERVINGS.

1½ cups wheat berries (whole-grain wheat)
1 bunch (10 to 12 ounces) spinach, tough stems trimmed
1 medium tomato
10 dried tomato halves (about 1 ounce)
3 tablespoons olive oil

2 tablespoons red wine vinegar
½ teaspoon Dijon mustard
1 teaspoon salt
½ teaspoon sugar
¼ teaspoon coarsely ground black pepper
1 cup golden raisins

1. In large bowl, soak wheat berries overnight in enough *water* to cover by 2 inches.

2. Drain wheat berries. In 4-quart saucepan, heat *7 cups water* to boiling over high heat. Add soaked wheat berries; heat to boiling. Reduce heat to low; cover and simmer until wheat berries are tender, about 1 hour. Drain.

3. Meanwhile, coarsely chop spinach. Chop tomato. Place dried tomato halves in small bowl; add *1 cup boiling water*. Let stand 5 minutes; drain well. Coarsely chop dried tomatoes.

4. Prepare dressing: In medium bowl, with wire whisk or fork, mix oil, vinegar, mustard, salt, sugar, and pepper until blended. Add raisins, diced tomato, chopped dried tomatoes, spinach, and wheat berries; toss well.

Each serving: About 455 calories, 12g protein, 82g carbohydrate, 12g total fat (1g saturated), 0mg cholesterol, 625mg sodium.

Penne with Green Beans and Basil

Penne with Green Beans and Basil

This cool pasta salad is perfect for a hot night.

PREP: 15 MINUTES COOK: 20 MINUTES
MAKES 8 CUPS OR 4 MAIN-DISH SERVINGS.

8 ounces penne or bow-tie pasta
1 pound green beans, trimmed and
 each cut in half
1¹/₂ teaspoons salt
1 tablespoon water
1 cup loosely packed fresh
 basil leaves

¹/₄ cup extravirgin olive oil
¹/₂ teaspoon coarsely ground
 black pepper
1 medium tomato, chopped
small basil leaves for garnish

1. In large saucepot, cook penne as label directs.

2. Meanwhile, in 12-inch skillet, heat *1 inch water* to boiling over high heat. Add green beans and ¹/₂ teaspoon salt; heat to boiling. Cook beans until tender-crisp, 8 to 10 minutes. Drain beans. Rinse beans under cold running water to cool slightly; drain again.

3. In blender at high speed, combine basil, oil, and water and puree until almost smooth, stopping blender occasionally and scraping down sides with rubber spatula. Transfer basil puree to large bowl; stir in remaining 1 teaspoon salt and pepper.

4. Drain pasta; rinse under cold running water and drain again. In warm serving bowl, toss pasta, beans, tomato, and basil puree. Garnish with basil leaves.

Each serving: About 370 calories, 10g protein, 52g carbohydrate, 15g total fat (2g saturated), 0mg cholesterol, 680mg sodium.

Rice Noodles with Many Herbs

Whip up this light summer main dish with fast-cooking noodles, carrots, cucumber, herbs, and our delicious Asian dressing. Serve warm or at room temperature.

PREP: 20 MINUTES   COOK: 10 MINUTES
MAKES 4 MAIN-DISH SERVINGS.

3 small carrots, peeled and cut
　into 2" by 1/4" matchstick strips
　(1 1/3 cups)
1/3 cup seasoned rice vinegar
1 package (1 pound) 1/2-inch-wide
　flat rice noodles
1/3 English (seedless) cucumber,
　unpeeled and cut into 2" by 1/4"
　matchstick strips (1 cup)

1 cup loosely packed fresh
　cilantro leaves
1/2 cup loosely packed fresh
　mint leaves
1/3 cup loosely packed small fresh
　basil leaves
1/3 cup snipped fresh chives
2 teaspoons Asian sesame oil

1. In small bowl, stir carrots with rice vinegar. Let stand at room temperature while preparing noodles.
2. In 8-quart saucepot, heat *5 quarts water* to boiling over high heat. Add noodles and cook just until cooked through, about 3 minutes. Drain noodles; rinse under cold running water and drain again.
3. Transfer noodles to large shallow serving bowl. Add carrots with their liquid, cucumber, cilantro, mint, basil, chives, and sesame oil; toss well.

Each serving: About 470 calories, 7g protein, 105g carbohydrate,
3g total fat (0g saturated), 0mg cholesterol, 550mg sodium.

Rice Noodles with Many Herbs

Pasta Toss with Summer Basil

Use any short pasta for this delicious dish that is full of garden-fresh vegetables. If you like, you can substitute yellow summer squash for all or part of the zucchini.

PREP: 45 MINUTES   COOK: 35 MINUTES
MAKES 4 MAIN-DISH SERVINGS.

3 medium red peppers
2 medium yellow peppers
1 package (16 ounces) penne,
   radiatore, or fusilli pasta
4 tablespoons olive oil
1 medium red onion, chopped
3 medium zucchini (6 ounces each),
   each cut lengthwise in half then
   thinly sliced crosswise

1 medium eggplant (1^1/$_4$ pounds),
   cut into ^{1}/$_2$-inch pieces
1^1/$_4$ teaspoons salt
3 ripe medium tomatoes (1 pound),
   chopped
1 cup loosely packed fresh basil
   leaves, chopped (^{1}/$_2$ cup)
2 tablespoons capers, drained

1. Preheat broiler. Line broiling pan with foil. Cut each pepper lengthwise in half; remove and discard stems and seeds. Arrange peppers (half at a time, if broiling pan is small), cut side down, in prepared broiling pan. With hand, flatten each pepper half. Place pan in broiler 5 to 6 inches from heat source. Broil until charred and blistered, 8 to 10 minutes. Wrap peppers in foil and allow to steam at room temperature until cool enough to handle, about 15 minutes. (Repeat with remaining peppers.)

2. Meanwhile, in large saucepot, cook pasta as label directs. Drain pasta; rinse with cold water and drain again. Set aside.

3. Remove peppers from foil. Peel off skin and discard. Cut peppers into ^{1}/$_2$-inch pieces.

4. In nonstick 12-inch skillet, heat 1 tablespoon oil over medium heat until hot. Add the onion and cook, stirring occasionally, until tender, about 6 minutes. Add zucchini and 1 tablespoon oil, and cook, stirring frequently, until zucchini are tender-crisp, about 7 minutes. Add eggplant, 3/4 teaspoon salt, and remaining 2 tablespoons oil and cook, stirring frequently, until eggplant is tender, about 8 minutes.

5. Transfer vegetables to large bowl; stir in tomatoes, basil, capers, and remaining 1/2 teaspoon salt. Add pasta; toss well. Serve salad warm or cover and refrigerate until ready to serve.

Each serving: About 675 calories, 21g protein, 114g carbohydrate, 18g total fat (3g saturated), 0mg cholesterol, 855mg sodium.

Tomato and Orzo Salad

This perfect pasta toss requires little cooking but yields big flavor.

PREP: 20 MINUTES   COOK: 8 MINUTES
MAKES ABOUT 7 1/2 CUPS OR 4 MAIN-DISH SERVINGS.

salt
1 1/4 cups orzo pasta
1/2 pound green beans, trimmed and
  each cut into thirds
2 large lemons
2 tablespoons extravirgin olive oil
2 teaspoons fresh oregano leaves,
  chopped

1/4 teaspoon coarsely ground
  black pepper
1 pound ripe tomatoes (about 3
  medium), cut into 1/2-inch pieces
4 ounces ricotta salata cheese,
  crumbled, or Parmesan cheese,
  shaved

1. In 4-quart saucepan, heat *3 quarts of salted water* to boiling over high heat. Add orzo; heat to boiling and cook 4 minutes. Add green beans and cook until orzo and beans are tender, about 4 minutes longer. Drain well.
2. Meanwhile, from lemons, grate 1 teaspoon peel and squeeze 1/4 cup juice. In large bowl, with wire whisk or fork, mix oil, oregano, 3/4 teaspoon salt, pepper, and lemon peel and juice until blended.
3. Add warm orzo and beans to dressing in bowl and toss well. Gently stir in tomatoes and ricotta salata.

Each serving: About 340 calories, 12g protein, 44g carbohydrate, 14g total fat (6g saturated), 26mg cholesterol, 1,010mg sodium.

Fattoush

This Lebanese salad is packed with juicy summer-ripe tomatoes and fresh herbs. Pieces of toasted pita absorb the tasty dressing.

PREP: 25 MINUTES PLUS STANDING
MAKES ABOUT 16 CUPS OR 4 MAIN-DISH SERVINGS.

3 tablespoons fresh lemon juice
3 tablespoons olive oil
1 teaspoon salt
1/2 teaspoon coarsely ground
   black pepper
4 medium tomatoes (about 1 1/4
   pounds), cut into 1/2-inch pieces
3 green onions, trimmed and chopped
1 medium cucumber (8 ounces),
   peeled, seeded, and cut into
   1/2-inch pieces

1 cup loosely packed fresh
   parsley leaves
1/2 cup loosely packed fresh
   mint leaves, chopped
4 (6-inch) pitas, each split
   horizontally in half
1 small head romaine lettuce (about
   1 pound), coarsely chopped

1. In large salad bowl, with wire whisk or fork, mix lemon juice, oil, salt, and pepper. Add tomatoes, green onions, cucumber, parsley, and mint; toss to coat. Let tomato mixture stand 15 minutes to allow flavors to blend.
2. Meanwhile, toast pitas; cool. Break pitas into 1-inch pieces.
3. Just before serving, toss lettuce and pitas with tomato mixture.

Each serving: About 315 calories, 9g protein, 47g carbohydrate, 12g total fat (2g saturated), 0mg cholesterol, 935mg sodium.

Greek Pasta Toss

Greek Pasta Toss

A great Greek salad (minus the lettuce) with hot pasta and beans folded in makes a complete meal.

PREP: 25 MINUTES   COOK: 15 MINUTES
MAKES 6 MAIN-DISH SERVINGS.

1 pound rotini or fusilli pasta
1/4 cup olive oil
2 tablespoons balsamic vinegar
1 garlic clove, crushed with garlic press
1/2 teaspoon salt
1/4 teaspoon coarsely ground black pepper
9 ripe medium tomatoes (about 3 pounds), cut into thin wedges
2 cans (15 to 19 ounces each) garbanzo beans, rinsed and drained

8 ounces feta cheese, coarsely crumbled
2 Kirby cucumbers (about 4 ounces each), unpeeled and cut into 1/4-inch pieces
1/2 cup Kalamata olives, pitted and chopped
1/2 cup packed fresh parsley leaves, chopped
1/2 cup packed fresh dill, chopped

1. In large saucepot, cook pasta as label directs.
2. Meanwhile, in large serving bowl, with wire whisk, mix oil, vinegar, garlic, salt, and pepper until blended. Add tomatoes, beans, feta, cucumbers, olives, parsley, and dill. Toss until evenly mixed and coated with dressing.
3. Drain pasta. Add pasta to tomato mixture in bowl; toss well.

Each serving: About 685 calories, 26g protein, 97g carbohydrate, 22g total fat (8g saturated), 34mg cholesterol, 1,154mg sodium.

Greek Peasant Salad

Serve this cool Mediterranean-style on a summer night.

PREP: 25 MINUTES

MAKES ABOUT 6 1/2 CUPS OR 4 MAIN-DISH SERVINGS.

4 Kirby cucumbers (about 1 pound)
2 tablespoons fresh lemon juice
1 tablespoon olive oil
1/4 teaspoon salt
1/8 teaspoon ground black pepper
2 pounds ripe red and/or yellow tomatoes (about 6 medium), cut into 1-inch pieces

1/2 cup loosely packed fresh mint leaves, chopped
1/3 cup Kalamata olives, pitted and coarsely chopped
1/4 cup loosely packed fresh dill, chopped
2 ounces feta cheese, crumbled (1/2 cup)

1. With vegetable peeler, remove 3 or 4 evenly spaced lengthwise strips of peel from each cucumber. Cut each cucumber lengthwise into quarters, then crosswise into 1/2-inch pieces.

2. In large bowl, with wire whisk or fork, mix lemon juice, oil, salt, and pepper until blended. Add cucumbers, tomatoes, mint, olives, and dill, and toss until evenly mixed and coated with dressing. Top with feta.

Each serving: About 150 calories, 5g protein, 17g carbohydrate, 9g total fat (3g saturated), 12mg cholesterol, 42g sodium.

Greek Peasant Salad

Flatbread with Salad

Try this salad "pizza" as an alternative to the usual tomato-and-cheese kind. It's especially good because it starts with our excellent crusty Grilled Flatbread.

PREP: 20 MINUTES PLUS PREPARATION OF FLATBREADS
MAKES 4 MAIN-DISH SERVINGS.

GRILLED FLATBREAD
1 package active dry yeast
1 teaspoon sugar
1¼ cups warm water (105°F to 115°F)
about 4 cups all-purpose flour
about 3 tablespoons olive oil
2 teaspoons salt

SALAD
2 tablespoons extravirgin olive oil
2 tablespoons red wine vinegar

1 teaspoon sugar
1 teaspoon Dijon mustard
¼ teaspoon salt
⅛ teaspoon ground black pepper
6 cups salad greens, such as radicchio, endive, and arugula, torn into ½-inch pieces
2 ripe medium tomatoes, cut into ½-inch pieces
1 small cucumber, peeled and cut into ½-inch pieces

1. Prepare flatbread: In large bowl, combine yeast, sugar, and ¼ cup warm water; stir to dissolve. Let stand until foamy, about 5 minutes. With a wooden spoon, stir in 1½ cups flour, 2 tablespoons olive oil, salt, and remaining 1 cup warm water until blended. With spoon, gradually stir in 2 cups flour. With floured hand, knead mixture in bowl to combine.

2. Turn dough onto lightly floured surface and knead, working in more flour (about ½ cup), until smooth and elastic, about 10 minutes.

3. Shape dough into ball and place in greased large bowl, turning to grease top. Cover bowl with plastic wrap and let rise in warm place (80°F to 85°F) until doubled in volume, about 1 hour. (After dough has risen, if not using dough right away, punch down and leave in bowl, cover loosely with greased plastic wrap, and refrigerate until ready to use, up to 24 hours. When ready to use, follow directions below.)

4. Punch down dough. Turn dough onto lightly floured surface. Cover and let rest 15 minutes.

5. Meanwhile, prepare grill. Grease two large cookie sheets.

6. Shape dough into 4 balls. On lightly floured surface, with floured rolling pin, roll 1 dough ball at a time into 12-inch round about ⅛ inch thick. (The diameter or shape of round is not as important as even thick-

Flatbread with Salad

ness.) Place rounds on prepared cookie sheets; lightly brush tops with some remaining oil.

7. About 10 minutes before grilling flatbread, prepare salad topping: In large bowl, with wire whisk, mix oil, vinegar, sugar, mustard, salt, and pepper until blended. Add salad greens, tomatoes, and cucumber; toss to coat well. Set aside.

8. With hands, place 1 round at a time, greased side down, on hot grill rack over medium heat. Grill until grill marks appear on underside and dough stiffens (dough may puff slightly), 2 to 3 minutes. Brush top with some oil. With tongs, turn bread and grill until grill marks appear on underside and bread is cooked through, 2 to 3 minutes longer. Transfer flatbread to tray; keep warm. Repeat with remaining dough rounds.

9. To serve, top each flatbread with about 2 cups salad. Cut each round into quarters. Serve 4 wedges per person.

Each serving of flatbread: About 370 calories, 10g protein, 64g carbohydrate, 8g total fat (2g saturated), 0mg cholesterol, 610mg sodium.

Each serving of flatbread with salad: About 620 calories, 16g protein, 106g carbohydrate, 14g total fat (2g saturated), 0mg cholesterol, 1,250mg sodium.

Szechuan Peanut-Noodle Salad

A tasty pasta salad packed with great Asian flavors. To serve cold, chill the pasta and toss with the vegetables just before serving.

PREP: 25 MINUTES   COOK: 25 MINUTES
MAKES 5 MAIN-DISH SERVINGS.

1 package (16 ounces) linguine or spaghetti
2 1/2 teaspoons salt
4 ounces snow peas, strings removed
1/2 cup creamy peanut butter
1 tablespoon grated, peeled fresh ginger
1/4 cup soy sauce
2 tablespoons distilled white vinegar
2 teaspoons Asian sesame oil
1/4 teaspoon hot pepper sauce
1 small cucumber (6 ounces), peeled, seeded, and cut into 2" by 1/4" matchstick strips
1/4 cup dry-roasted peanuts
1 green onion, trimmed and chopped

1. In large saucepot, cook linguine as label directs, using 2 teaspoons salt.
2. Meanwhile, in 3-quart saucepan, heat *1 inch water* to boiling; add snow peas. Reduce heat and simmer 2 minutes; drain. Rinse with cold running water; drain. Cut snow peas lengthwise into 1/4-inch-wide matchstick strips; set aside.
3. Drain linguine, reserving 1 cup pasta water.
4. Prepare dressing: In large bowl, with wire whisk, mix peanut butter, ginger, reserved pasta water, soy sauce, vinegar, sesame oil, hot pepper sauce, and remaining 1/2 teaspoon salt until smooth.
5. Add linguine to dressing in bowl and toss to coat. Add snow peas and cucumber; toss to combine. Sprinkle with peanuts and green onion.

Each serving: About 572 calories, 22g protein, 78g carbohydrate, 20g total fat (3g saturated), 0mg cholesterol, 1,794mg sodium.

Tofu "Egg" Salad

A real surprise! Looks and tastes just like egg salad but has no cholesterol. Enjoy it on its own or make into sandwiches on whole-grain bread with sliced tomato and crisp lettuce.

PREP: 15 MINUTES
MAKES 4 MAIN-DISH SERVINGS.

**1 package (16 ounces) firm or
    extrafirm tofu, drained**
1 medium stalk celery, chopped
1/2 small red pepper, chopped
1 green onion, trimmed and chopped

1/4 cup light mayonnaise
1/2 teaspoon Dijon mustard
1/2 teaspoon salt
1/8 teaspoon turmeric

In medium bowl, with fork, mash tofu until it resembles scrambled eggs. Stir in celery, red pepper, green onion, mayonnaise, mustard, salt, and tumeric. Cover and refrigerate if not serving right away.

Each serving: About 195 calories, 18g protein, 10g carbohydrate, 11g total fat (1g saturated), 0mg cholesterol, 445mg sodium.

Egg Salad Deluxe

Hard-cooked eggs are chopped and mixed with sautéed onions, mushrooms, and celery for a new take on the classic egg salad. If you like, serve with toasted whole-grain bread.

PREP: 20 MINUTES   COOK: 20 MINUTES
MAKES ABOUT 4 1/2 CUPS OR 6 MAIN-DISH SERVINGS.

8 large eggs
3 tablespoons olive oil
1 medium onion, cut in half and thinly sliced
10 ounces mushrooms, sliced
2 medium stalks celery, finely chopped

1/4 cup loosely packed fresh parsley leaves, chopped
1/2 teaspoon salt
1/4 teaspoon coarsely ground black pepper
1 head Boston lettuce, leaves separated

1. In 3-quart saucepan, place eggs and enough *cold water* to cover by at least 1 inch; heat to boiling over high heat. Immediately remove saucepan from heat and cover tightly; let stand 15 minutes. Pour off hot water and run cold water over eggs until easy to handle.

2. Meanwhile, in nonstick 12-inch skillet, heat 1 tablespoon oil over medium heat until hot. Add onion and cook, stirring occasionally, until tender and golden, 10 to 12 minutes. Increase heat to medium-high; add mushrooms and cook until mushrooms are golden and all liquid has evaporated, about 8 minutes.

3. Peel hard-cooked eggs and finely chop. In large bowl, combine eggs with mushroom mixture, celery, parsley, salt, pepper, and remaining 2 tablespoons oil; toss well.

4. To serve, line platter with lettuce leaves and top with egg salad.

Each serving: About 190 calories, 11g protein, 5g carbohydrate, 14g total fat (3g saturated), 283mg cholesterol, 290mg sodium.

Provençal Pasta Salad

The robust flavors of this colorful salad—complete with eggplant, tomatoes, garlic, basil, and olives—will transport you and your guests to sunny southern France.

PREP: 30 MINUTES   COOK: 30 MINUTES
MAKES ABOUT 12 CUPS OR 6 MAIN-DISH SERVINGS.

12 ounces bow-tie pasta
2 medium red peppers or 1 jar
   (7 ounces) roasted red peppers,
   drained and cut into 1/2-inch pieces
2 tablespoons olive oil
1 medium onion, chopped
1 small eggplant (about 3/4 pound),
   cut into 1/2-inch pieces
2 garlic cloves, minced

3/4 teaspoon salt
1/4 teaspoon coarsely ground
   black pepper
1 pint cherry tomatoes, each cut
   in half
1 cup loosely packed fresh basil
   leaves, coarsely chopped
1/3 cup Kalamata olives, pitted
   and coarsely chopped

1. In large saucepot, cook pasta as label directs. Reserve 1/4 cup pasta water. Drain and rinse pasta under cold running water; drain again.

2. Meanwhile, roast peppers if using fresh ones: Preheat broiler. Line broiling pan with foil. Cut each pepper lengthwise in half; remove and discard stems and seeds. Arrange peppers, cut side down, in prepared pan. With hand, flatten each pepper half. Place pan in broiler 5 to 6 inches from heat source. Broil until skin is charred and blistered, 8 to 10 minutes. Wrap peppers in foil and allow to steam at room temperature until cool enough to handle, about 15 minutes. Remove peppers from foil. Peel off skin and discard. Cut peppers into 1/2-inch pieces.

3. In nonstick 12-inch skillet, heat oil over medium heat until hot. Add onion and cook, stirring often, until tender and golden, about 10 minutes. Increase heat to medium-high. Add eggplant, garlic, salt, and black pepper and cook, stirring often, until eggplant is tender and golden, about 8 minutes longer.

4. To pasta, add roasted peppers, onion mixture, tomatoes, basil, olives, and reserved pasta water; toss gently. Transfer pasta mixture to serving bowl. Cover and refrigerate if not serving right away.

Each serving: About 300 calories, 9g protein, 52g carbohydrate, 7g total fat (1g saturated), 0mg cholesterol, 495mg sodium.

QUICK
DINNERS

Spinach Soufflé

We all live hectic lives today. Few of us have time to spend hours preparing from-scratch meals seven days a week. Even if we did have the time, there are thousands of other things competing for each extra minute. So in this chapter, we've put together a collection of scrumptious meatless recipes that require the bare minimum of muss, fuss, labor—perfect for busy households.

What's the secret? Making smart use of convenience foods and staples from the pantry and refrigerator, then adding your own vegetables, herbs, and spices. In no more than forty minutes you can have any of the dishes in this chapter on the table and ready to eat. These are not mere thrown-together, ho-hum meals either. They are wholesome, satisfying vegetarian dishes that everyone will find delicious.

Ample use is made of canned beans and tomato products, quick-cooking grains and pasta, jars of olives and salsa, packaged shredded cheeses, and bags of precut vegetables. Eggs are the basis of an airy spinach soufflé and several savory frittatas; black beans take center stage in burgers, burritos, and chili; vegetables abound in Barley-Vegetable Stew, Tofu Stir-fry, and Vegetarian Tortilla Pie. Pasta recipes show off myriad shapes and sizes: Pasta Ribbons with Chunky Vegetables; Fusilli with Garbanzo Beans and Spinach; Bow Ties with Tomatoes, Herbs, and Lemon; Cavatelli with Ricotta and Fresh Tomato Sauce are but a few.

Cuisines from around the world offer many palate-pleasing vegetarian recipes. Most supermarkets, specialty food shops, and markets stock a wide array of ethnic products that can easily be stored in your pantry for quick and hassle-free dinners. From the recipes in this chapter, you can sample the flavors of the Middle East with our zesty Falafel Cones, a traditional snack. Try spicy cheese-and-vegetable-filled Queso-Blanco Soft Tacos for a taste of Mexico. Skillet Vegetable Curry is infused with the exotic spices of India. And, we've streamlined the Polish specialty, Pierogi and Sauerkraut-Slaw Casserole, with frozen pierogies and pre-cut cabbage.

Another great feature of the time-saving nature of these dishes is that few pots and pans are used in preparation. That means cleanup is a breeze, allowing you to spend more time with your family, which is, after all, the most valuable use of your time.

Black Bean and Sweet Potato Chili

This hearty chili is great for cool nights in early fall. Try it with pinto, cannellini, kidney, or pink beans, or use a combination of beans for a colorful entrée.

PREP: 10 MINUTES   COOK: 20 MINUTES
MAKES ABOUT 10 CUPS OR 4 MAIN-DISH SERVINGS.

1 tablespoon olive oil	1 jar (16 ounces) mild salsa
1 medium onion, chopped	1 cup water
2 garlic cloves, chopped	2 cans (15 to 19 ounces each)
2 medium sweet potatoes (about 12	low-sodium black beans
ounces each), peeled and cut into	1/2 cup reduced-fat sour cream
1/2-inch pieces	1/4 cup loosely packed fresh cilantro
1 tablespoon chili powder	leaves, chopped

1. In 4-quart saucepan, heat oil over medium-high heat until hot. Add onion and garlic; cook, stirring occasionally, until soft, 4 minutes. Stir in sweet potatoes, chili powder, salsa, and water; heat to boiling. Reduce heat to medium-low and cook, stirring occasionally, until potatoes are fork-tender, 12 to 15 minutes. Add beans with their liquid and cook 3 minutes longer.

2. In small bowl, with fork, stir sour cream and cilantro to combine. Serve chili with cilantro cream.

Each serving: About 520 calories, 23g protein, 91g carbohydrate, 9g total fat (3g saturated) 12mg cholesterol, 950mg sodium.

Southwestern Black Bean Burgers

For a second easy weeknight meal, make a double batch and freeze the uncooked burgers. Defrost 10 minutes, then cook, turning once, until heated through, about 12 minutes.

PREP: 10 MINUTES   COOK: 6 MINUTES
MAKES 4 SANDWICHES.

1 can (15 to 19 ounces) black beans, rinsed and drained
2 tablespoons light mayonnaise
1/4 cup packed fresh cilantro leaves, chopped
1 tablespoon plain dried bread crumbs
1/2 teaspoon ground cumin
1/2 teaspoon hot pepper sauce
nonstick cooking spray
1 cup loosely packed sliced lettuce
4 mini (4-inch) whole-wheat pitas, warmed
1/2 cup mild salsa

1. In large bowl, with potato masher or fork, mash beans with mayonnaise until almost smooth with some lumps. Stir in cilantro, bread crumbs, cumin, and pepper sauce until combined. With lightly floured hands, shape bean mixture into four 3-inch round patties. Spray both sides of each patty lightly with nonstick cooking spray.

2. Heat 10-inch skillet over medium heat until hot. Add patties and cook until lightly browned, about 3 minutes. With pancake turner, turn patties over, and cook until heated through, 3 minutes longer.

3. Arrange lettuce on pitas; top with burgers then salsa.

Each sandwich: About 210 calories, 13g protein, 42g carbohydrate, 3g total fat (0g saturated), 0mg cholesterol, 715mg sodium.

Southwestern Black Bean Burgers

Couscous with Garbanzo Beans

Couscous with Garbanzo Beans

A vegetarian entrée fragrant with the flavors of Morocco—warm spices, green olives, and garlic—gets a quick start from preseasoned couscous mix.

PREP: 5 MINUTES   COOK: 10 MINUTES
MAKES 4 MAIN-DISH SERVINGS.

1 box (5.6 ounces) couscous (Moroccan pasta) with toasted pine nuts
1/3 cup dark seedless raisins
1 tablespoon olive oil
1 medium zucchini (about 10 ounces), cut lengthwise in half, then crosswise into 1/2-inch-thick slices
1 garlic clove, crushed with garlic press

3/4 teaspoon ground cumin
3/4 teaspoon ground coriander
1/8 teaspoon ground red pepper (cayenne)
2 cans (15 to 19 ounces each) garbanzo beans, rinsed and drained
1/2 cup salad olives, drained, or chopped pimiento-stuffed olives
1/4 cup water

1. Prepare couscous as label directs, except add raisins to cooking water.
2. Meanwhile, in nonstick 12-inch skillet, heat oil over medium-high heat until hot. Add zucchini and cook, stirring occasionally, 5 minutes. Add garlic, cumin, coriander, and red pepper and cook, stirring, 30 seconds. Add beans, olives, and water and cook, stirring often, until heated through, about 5 minutes.
3. Add cooked couscous to bean mixture and toss gently. Spoon into serving bowl.

Each serving: About 555 calories, 20g protein, 101g carbohydrate, 10g total fat (1g saturated), 0mg cholesterol, 1,110mg sodium.

Fast Fried Rice

The secrets to this dish are quick-cooking brown rice, precut frozen vegetables, and ready-to-use stir-fry sauce.

PREP: 5 MINUTES COOK: 15 MINUTES
MAKES 4 MAIN-DISH SERVINGS.

1½ cups quick-cooking brown rice
1 pound firm tofu, drained and cut
   into 1-inch cubes
6 teaspoons olive oil
1 package (16 ounces) frozen
   vegetables for stir-fry

2 large eggs, lightly beaten
⅓ cup stir-fry sauce
¼ cup water

1. Prepare rice as label directs.
2. Meanwhile, in medium bowl, place 3 layers paper towels. Place tofu on towels and top with 3 more layers paper towels. With hand, gently press tofu to extract excess moisture.
3. In nonstick 12-inch skillet, heat 2 teaspoons oil over medium-high heat until hot. Add frozen vegetables; cover and cook, stirring occasionally, 5 minutes. Transfer vegetables to bowl; keep warm.
4. In same skillet, heat remaining 4 teaspoons oil until hot. Add tofu and cook, stirring gently, 5 minutes. Stir in cooked rice and cook 4 minutes longer.
5. With spatula, push rice mixture around edge of skillet, leaving space in center. Add eggs to center of skillet; cook, stirring eggs until scrambled, about 1 minute. Add stir-fry sauce, vegetables, and water; cook, stirring, 1 minute.

Each serving: About 360 calories, 17g protein, 41g carbohydrate, 15g total fat (2g saturated), 106mg cholesterol, 760mg sodium.

Fast Fried Rice

Fusilli with Garbanzo Beans and Spinach

Fusilli with Garbanzo Beans and Spinach

A staple of Italian cuisine, beans show up almost everywhere, including pasta dishes. For this dish, we use canned garbanzo beans to reduce preparation and cooking time.

PREP: 8 MINUTES   COOK: 12 MINUTES
MAKES 6 MAIN-DISH SERVINGS.

1 pound fusilli pasta
2 tablespoons olive oil
1 medium onion, chopped
2 garlic cloves, crushed with garlic press
1/2 teaspoon dried oregano
1 can (29 ounces) garbanzo beans,

rinsed and drained
3 tablespoons balsamic vinegar
1 1/4 teaspoons salt
1/4 teaspoon coarsely ground black pepper
2 bags (6 ounces each) baby spinach

1. In large saucepot, cook pasta as label directs.

2. Meanwhile, in 12-inch skillet, heat oil over medium-high heat until hot. Add onion; cook, covered, 5 minutes, stirring often. Stir in garlic and oregano and cook 30 seconds. Stir in beans, vinegar, salt, and pepper; cook, stirring often, 5 minutes.

3. Drain pasta, reserving 1 cup pasta water. Return pasta to saucepot. Add spinach, bean mixture, and reserved pasta water; toss gently to combine.

Each serving: About 500 calories, 20g protein, 85g carbohydrate, 8g total fat (1g saturated), 0mg cholesterol, 980mg sodium.

Black Bean and Corn Burritos

These hearty burritos are an excellent choice for people on the go. Mexican-blend cheese is a mixture of Cheddar and Monterey Jack cheeses. If unavailable, substitute either of the cheeses.

PREP: 10 MINUTES   COOK: 5 MINUTES

MAKES 4 MAIN-DISH SERVINGS.

2 teaspoons chili powder

1 can (15 to 19 ounces) black beans, rinsed, drained, and coarsely mashed

1 can (15¼ ounces) whole-kernel corn, drained

3 tablespoons sliced pickled jalapeño chiles, drained and chopped (optional)

4 burrito-size flour tortillas, warmed

2 cups thinly sliced or chopped lettuce

2 medium tomatoes, chopped

1 cup shredded Mexican-blend cheese

sour cream (optional)

1. In 3-quart saucepan, toast chili powder over medium heat until fragrant, about 1 minute. Stir in black beans, corn, and jalapeño chiles; cook, stirring occasionally, until mixture is hot, 3 to 4 minutes.

2. Spoon one-fourth of bean mixture into center of each tortilla; top each with one-fourth of lettuce, tomatoes, and cheese. Fold two opposite sides of each tortilla over filling, then fold over other sides to form a package. Serve with sour cream, if you like.

Each serving without sour cream: About 490 calories, 20g protein, 75g carbohydrate, 15g total fat (7g saturated), 25mg cholesterol, 985mg sodium.

Pasta with Eggplant Sauce

Leftovers from our Eggplant Parmesan make a quick weeknight pasta supper. Serve this easy pasta toss with mixed greens and crusty bread.

PREP: 5 MINUTES   COOK: 25 MINUTES
MAKES 4 MAIN-DISH SERVINGS.

1 package (16 ounces) rigatoni or
    fusilli pasta
2 cups Tomato Sauce reserved from
    Eggplant Parmesan (page 208)

1 quarter (about 6" by 4" piece)
    reserved Eggplant Parmesan (page
    208) cut into 3/4-inch pieces (about
    2 1/2 cups)

1. In large saucepot, cook pasta as label directs.
2. Meanwhile, in 2-quart saucepan, heat Tomato Sauce and cut-up Eggplant Parmesan over medium heat, stirring occasionally, until hot, about 15 minutes.
3. Drain pasta, reserving 1/4 cup pasta water. Return pasta to saucepot; add eggplant mixture and reserved pasta water and toss well.

Each serving: About 615 calories, 24g protein, 107g carbohydrate, 10g total fat (3g saturated), 15mg cholesterol, 1,280mg sodium.

Cavatelli with Ricotta and Fresh Tomato Sauce

We used frozen cavatelli—a short, curled, rippled pasta. If you can't find it, substitute frozen gnocchi. Serve with mixed Italian salad greens and sesame breadsticks. Just before serving, toss the greens with olive oil and a squeeze of lemon juice.

PREP: 5 MINUTES   COOK: 25 MINUTES
MAKES 4 MAIN-DISH SERVINGS.

1 bag (16 ounces) frozen cavatelli
1 tablespoon olive oil
1 garlic clove, crushed with
   garlic press
4 medium tomatoes (about 1 1/2
   pounds), chopped

1/2 teaspoon salt
1/4 teaspoon coarsely ground
   black pepper
3/4 cup part-skim ricotta cheese
1/4 cup freshly grated Pecorino
   Romano or Parmesan cheese

1. In large saucepot, cook pasta as label directs.

2. Meanwhile, in nonstick 10-inch skillet, heat oil over medium heat until hot. Add garlic and cook, stirring, 1 minute. Stir in tomatoes, salt, and pepper and cook, stirring occasionally, until tomatoes break up slightly, about 5 minutes.

3. Drain cavatelli; transfer to warm serving bowl. Stir in ricotta and Romano. Pour tomato mixture on top; toss before serving.

Each serving: About 455 calories, 20g protein, 71g carbohydrate, 11g total fat (5g saturated), 40mg cholesterol, 560mg sodium.

Fettuccine with Creamy Tomato Sauce and Peas

Quick-cooking fresh pasta is tossed with chunky tomato sauce simmered with heavy cream.

PREP: 5 MINUTES   COOK: 15 MINUTES
MAKES 4 MAIN-DISH SERVINGS.

2 packages (9 ounces each) fresh
  (refrigerated) fettuccine
1 can (14 1/2 ounces) seasoned
  chunky tomatoes for pasta
1 can (15 ounces) tomato sauce

1/3 cup heavy or whipping cream
1 package (10 ounces) frozen peas
  freshly grated Parmesan cheese
  (optional)

1. In large saucepot, cook pasta as label directs.
2. Meanwhile, in 2-quart saucepan, heat tomatoes, tomato sauce, and cream to boiling over medium-high heat. Reduce heat to medium and cook, stirring, 2 minutes.
3. Place frozen peas in colander. Drain fettuccine over peas. In large warm serving bowl, toss fettuccine and peas with tomato mixture. Serve with Parmesan, if you like.

Each serving: About 575 calories, 22g protein, 96g carbohydrate, 13g total fat (6g saturated), 158mg cholesterol, 1,375mg sodium.

Bow Ties with Tomatoes, Herbs, and Lemon

The easy late-summer sauce "cooks" from the heat of the drained pasta. While the pasta boils, slice and warm a loaf of semolina bread for a simple go-along.

PREP: 15 MINUTES   COOK: 15 MINUTES
MAKES ABOUT 11 CUPS OR 4 MAIN-DISH SERVINGS.

6 medium tomatoes (about
  2 pounds), chopped
1/4 cup loosely packed fresh mint
  leaves, chopped
1/4 cup loosely packed fresh basil
  leaves, chopped
2 tablespoons olive oil

1 teaspoon grated lemon peel
1 garlic clove, crushed with
  garlic press
1 teaspoon salt
1/4 teaspoon ground black pepper
1 package (16 ounces) bow-tie or ziti
  pasta

1. In large serving bowl, stir tomatoes, mint, basil, olive oil, lemon peel, garlic, salt and pepper; set mixture aside to allow flavors to develop.
2. Meanwhile, in large saucepot, cook pasta as label directs. Drain well.
3. Add hot pasta to tomato mixture in bowl; toss well.

Each serving: About 530 calories, 17g protein, 96g carbohydrate, 9g total fat (1g saturated), 0mg cholesterol, 695mg sodium.

Broccoli Pesto Spaghetti

The pesto is best made in a food processor; a blender makes the mixture too creamy. Serve with breadsticks and a green salad splashed with balsamic vinegar.

PREP: 8 MINUTES   COOK: 12 MINUTES
MAKES ABOUT 8 CUPS OR 4 MAIN-DISH SERVINGS.

1 package (16 ounces) spaghetti
  or thin spaghetti
1 bag (16 ounces) frozen chopped
  broccoli
1 cup vegetable broth
1/4 cup freshly grated Parmesan
  cheese

2 tablespoons olive oil
1 small garlic clove
1/4 teaspoon salt
coarsely ground black pepper

1. In large saucepot, cook pasta as label directs. In saucepan, prepare broccoli as label directs.

2. In food processor, with knife blade attached, puree cooked broccoli, broth, Parmesan, oil, garlic, and salt until smooth, stopping processor occasionally to scrape down side.

3. Drain pasta; transfer to warm serving bowl. Add broccoli pesto to pasta; toss well. Sprinkle with pepper and serve.

Each serving: About 550 calories, 22g protein, 91g carbohydrate, 11g total fat (3g saturated), 5mg cholesterol, 615mg sodium.

Fettuccine with Mushrooms and Cream

Don't go out for pasta when you can whip up a hearty dish in your own kitchen. Sun-dried tomatoes and Marsala wine perk up this fettuccine and mushroom toss.

PREP: 15 MINUTES   COOK: 18 MINUTES
MAKES 4 MAIN-DISH SERVINGS.

2 packages (9 ounces each) refrigerated fettuccine pasta
1 tablespoon olive oil
1 small shallot, finely chopped (2 tablespoons)
8 ounces shiitake mushrooms, stems removed, and caps thinly sliced
8 ounces white mushrooms, trimmed and thinly sliced
1/2 teaspoon salt
1/4 cup Marsala wine
11/2 cups vegetable broth
1/3 cup heavy or whipping cream
1 cup loosely packed fresh basil or parsley leaves, chopped
1/4 cup sun-dried tomatoes in olive oil, sliced

1. In large saucepot, cook pasta as label directs.
2. Meanwhile, in nonstick 12-inch skillet, heat oil over medium-high heat until hot. Add shallot and cook, stirring occasionally, 1 minute. Add mushrooms and salt and cook, stirring occasionally, until tender and golden, 10 to 12 minutes.
3. Stir in the wine. Heat to boiling over medium-high heat and cook 1 minute. Add the broth and cream; heat to boiling and cook, stirring, 3 minutes.
4. Drain fettuccine and return to saucepot. Add mushroom mixture, basil, and sun-dried tomatoes and cook over medium heat, tossing until evenly coated, 1 minute.

Each serving: About 560 calories, 20g protein, 83g carbohydrate, 18g total fat (7g saturated), 158mg cholesterol, 815mg sodium.

Fettuccine with Mushrooms and Cream

Pasta Ribbons with Chunky Vegtables

Pasta Ribbons with Chunky Vegetables

Just as satisfying as lasagna but with half the work and half the time.

PREP: 10 MINUTES   COOK: 15 MINUTES
MAKES 4 MAIN-DISH SERVINGS.

salt
1 package (8 to 9 ounces) oven-
ready lasagna noodles (6 1/2" by
3 1/2" each)
1 tablespoon olive oil
2 medium yellow summer squash
and/or zucchini (10 ounces each),
cut into 3/4-inch-thick slices

1 package (10 ounces) mushrooms,
trimmed and cut into halves or
quarters, if large
2 cups tomato-basil pasta sauce
1/4 cup heavy or whipping cream
1 small chunk (2 ounces) Parmesan
cheese

1. In 4-quart saucepan, heat 3 quarts of *salted water* to boiling over high heat. Add lasagna noodles, 1 noodle at a time to avoid sticking; cook until tender, 7 to 8 minutes.

2. Meanwhile, in nonstick 12-inch skillet, heat oil over medium-high heat until very hot. Add squash and mushrooms; cover and cook, stirring occasionally, until vegetables are tender-crisp, 4 to 5 minutes. Add pasta sauce and cream; heat to boiling, stirring frequently.

3. Drain noodles. In serving bowl, toss noodles with squash mixture. With vegetable peeler, shave thin strips from Parmesan. Top pasta with Parmesan shavings to serve.

Each serving: About 515 calories, 19g protein, 70g carbohydrate, 18g total fat (7g saturated), 32mg cholesterol, 770mg sodium.

Poblano Rigatoni

Poblano Rigatoni

No need to fire up the grill. You'll get the same char-roasted flavor by searing the poblanos in a hot skillet—and you won't have to peel the chiles either!

PREP: 10 MINUTES COOK: 20 MINUTES
MAKES 4 MAIN-DISH SERVINGS.

1 package (16 ounces) rigatoni pasta
1 tablespoon olive oil
3 poblano chiles (8 ounces) or 2 large green peppers, cut into 1/2-inch strips
1 small onion, cut into 1/2-inch-thick slices
2 small zucchini (about 6 ounces each), cut into 1/2-inch-thick slices

2 garlic cloves, crushed with garlic press
1/2 teaspoon dried oregano, crumbled
1 teaspoon salt
1 pint grape or cherry tomatoes
4 ounces Monterey Jack cheese, cut into 1/2-inch pieces

1. In large saucepot, cook pasta as label directs.
2. Meanwhile, in nonstick 12-inch skillet, heat oil over medium-high heat until hot. Add chiles and onion; cook until lightly charred and tender-crisp, about 7 minutes. Add zucchini; cover and cook 3 minutes. Add garlic, oregano, and salt; cook 30 seconds. Stir in tomatoes; cover and cook until slightly softened.
3. Drain pasta. In serving bowl, toss pasta with vegetables and cheese.

Each serving: About 635 calories, 25g protein, 100g carbohydrate, 15g total fat (7g saturated), 30mg cholesterol, 925mg sodium.

Spinach Soufflé

Even though this recipe requires about 40 minutes total, only 20 minutes are active prep. During the remaining 20 minutes, while the soufflé bakes, you can relax! Serve with crusty rolls and a salad of mixed baby greens.

PREP: 20 MINUTES   BAKE: 20 MINUTES
MAKES 4 MAIN-DISH SERVINGS.

3 tablespoons plain dried bread crumbs

1 1/2 cups low-fat milk (1%)

1/3 cup cornstarch

2 large eggs, separated

1 package (10 ounces) frozen chopped spinach, thawed and squeezed dry

3 tablespoons freshly grated Parmesan cheese

1/2 teaspoon salt

1/4 teaspoon coarsely ground black pepper

1/2 teaspoon cream of tartar

4 large egg whites (see Tip below)

1. Preheat oven to 425°F. Spray 10-inch quiche dish or shallow 2-quart casserole with nonstick cooking spray; sprinkle with bread crumbs to coat. Set aside.

2. In 2-quart saucepan, with wire whisk, beat milk with cornstarch until blended. Heat milk mixture over medium-high heat, stirring constantly, until mixture thickens and boils; boil 1 minute. Remove pan from heat.

3. In large bowl, with rubber spatula, mix egg yolks, spinach, Parmesan, salt, and pepper until blended; stir in warm milk mixture. Cool slightly (if spinach mixture is too warm, it will deflate beaten egg whites).

4. In another large bowl, with mixer at high speed, beat cream of tartar and 6 egg whites until stiff peaks form. Gently fold egg-white mixture, one-third at a time, into spinach mixture.

5. Spoon soufflé mixture into quiche dish. Bake soufflé until top is golden and puffed, about 20 minutes. Serve immediately.

Each serving: About 195 calories, 15g protein, 23g carbohydrate, 5g total fat (2g saturated), 114mg cholesterol, 590mg sodium.

Tip

If you prefer, you can use liquid egg substitute or pasteurized liquid egg whites, which are sold in 1-pint containers in the dairy case of most supermarkets.

Spinach Soufflé

Herb and Feta Frittata

Packed with fresh herbs, this frittata is guaranteed to wake up any palate. Feel free to experiment by using your favorite fresh herbs: oregano, marjoram, or chervil to name just a few.

PREP: 15 MINUTES   BAKE: 15 MINUTES
MAKES 4 MAIN-DISH SERVINGS.

2 teaspoons olive oil
8 large eggs
4 ounces feta cheese, crumbled
1/3 cup loosely packed fresh parsley
   or basil leaves, chopped

1/4 cup whole milk
2 tablespoons fresh rosemary or
   thyme leaves, chopped
1/2 teaspoon ground black pepper

1. Preheat oven to 400°F. In oven-safe nonstick 10-inch skillet (if skillet is not oven-safe, wrap handle with double layer of foil), heat oil over medium heat until hot.

2. Meanwhile, in medium bowl, with wire whisk, beat eggs, feta, parsley, milk, rosemary, and pepper until blended. Pour egg mixture into skillet; do not stir. Cook until egg mixture begins to set around edge, 3 to 4 minutes.

3. Place skillet in oven; bake until frittata is set, 13 to 15 minutes. Cut frittata into wedges to serve.

Each serving: About 255 calories, 17g protein, 4g carbohydrate, 19g total fat (8g saturated), 452mg cholesterol, 450mg sodium.

Herb and Feta Frittata

Capellini Frittata

A satisfying meal made with sautéed onion and red pepper baked in an egg-and-pasta custard. If you have leftover spaghetti in the fridge, use 1 cup of it instead of the cooked capellini. Serve with a green salad, tossed with our Spicy Tomato Dressing (recipe follows) and a chunk of hearty peasant bread.

PREP: 14 MINUTES   BAKE: 6 MINUTES
MAKES 4 MAIN-DISH SERVINGS.

2 ounces capellini or angel hair
   pasta, broken into pieces
   (about 1/2 cup)
2 teaspoons olive oil
1 small onion, thinly sliced
1 small red pepper, chopped
6 large egg whites (see Tip page 148)

2 large eggs
1/3 cup freshly grated Parmesan
   cheese
1/4 cup fat-free (skim) milk
1/2 teaspoon salt
1/4 teaspoon hot pepper sauce

1. In 2-quart saucepan, heat *3 cups water* to boiling over high heat. Add pasta, and cook just until tender, about 2 minutes. Drain and set aside.

2. Meanwhile, preheat oven to 425°F. In oven-safe nonstick 10-inch skillet (if skillet is not oven-safe, wrap handle with double layer of foil), heat oil over medium heat. Add onion and red pepper and cook, stirring frequently, until tender, about 7 minutes.

3. In large bowl, with wire whisk or fork, beat egg whites, whole eggs, Parmesan, milk, salt, and hot pepper sauce; stir in pasta. Pour egg mixture over onion mixture; cover and cook until egg mixture is set around edge, about 3 minutes. Remove cover and place skillet in oven. Bake until frittata is set in center, about 6 minutes longer.

4. To serve, invert frittata onto warm serving plate, and cut into wedges.

Each serving: About 190 calories, 15g protein, 15g carbohydrate, 8g total fat (3g saturated), 113mg cholesterol, 545mg sodium.

Spicy Tomato Dressing

Made with vegetable juice and just a bit of olive oil, it's destined to be a new favorite.

Prep: 3 minutes
Makes about 1 cup.

1 can (5½ ounces) spicy-hot
  vegetable juice
3 tablespoons red wine vinegar
1 tablespoon olive oil

1 garlic clove, crushed with
  garlic press
½ teaspoon sugar
½ teaspoon dry mustard

In small bowl or jar, combine juice, vinegar, oil, garlic, sugar, and mustard. With wire whisk or fork, mix (or cover jar and shake) until blended. Cover and refrigerate. Stir or shake before using.

Each tablespoon: About 15 calories, 0g protein, 1g carbohydrate, 1g total fat (0g saturated), 0mg cholesterol, 35mg sodium.

Nacho Casserole

Warning: This soup-based casserole may become a family favorite! For less "heat," omit the jalapeños.

PREP: 10 MINUTES   BAKE: 20 MINUTES
MAKES 6 MAIN-DISH SERVINGS.

1 can (10 3/4 ounces) condensed
  Cheddar cheese soup
1/2 cup low-fat milk (1%)
1 jar (16 ounces) mild or medium-hot
  salsa
1 bag (7 ounces) baked, unsalted
  tortilla chips

1 can (16 ounces) fat-free refried
  beans
1 or 2 jalapeño chiles, thinly sliced
1 cup shredded Cheddar cheese

Preheat oven to 400°F. In 13" by 9" ceramic or glass baking dish, stir undiluted soup with milk until well blended; spread evenly. Top with half of salsa and half of chips. Carefully spread beans over chips. Top with remaining chips and salsa. Sprinkle evenly with chiles and Cheddar. Bake until hot, about 20 minutes.

Each serving: About 385 calories, 17g protein, 60g carbohydrate, 12g total fat (5g saturated), 27mg cholesterol, 1,370mg sodium.

Nacho Casserole

Mexican Potato Frittata

This flat, baked omelet combines a jar of salsa with a bit of sharp Cheddar cheese. Toss a package of prewashed baby spinach with sliced red onions, sliced fresh pears, and bottled salad dressing while the frittata bakes.

PREP: 20 MINUTES   BAKE: 5 MINUTES
MAKES 4 MAIN-DISH SERVINGS.

1 teaspoon olive oil
12 ounces red-skinned potatoes, cut
   into 1/2-inch pieces
6 large eggs
1 jar (11 to 12 ounces) medium-hot
   salsa

1/2 teaspoon salt
1/4 teaspoon coarsely ground
   black pepper
1/4 cup shredded sharp Cheddar
   cheese (1 ounce)
1 medium tomato

1. Preheat oven to 425°F. In oven-safe nonstick 10-inch skillet (if skillet is not oven-safe, wrap handle with double layer of foil), heat oil over medium-high heat until hot; add potatoes and cook, covered, until potatoes are tender and golden brown, about 10 minutes, stirring occasionally.

2. Meanwhile, in medium bowl, with wire whisk or fork, beat eggs with 1/4 cup salsa (chopped, if necessary), salt, and pepper. Stir in cheese; set aside. Chop tomato and stir into remaining salsa.

3. Stir egg mixture into potatoes in skillet and cook over medium heat, covered, until egg mixture begins to set around edge, about 3 minutes. Remove cover and place skillet in oven; bake until frittata is set, 4 to 6 minutes.

4. To serve, transfer frittata to cutting board. Cut into wedges and top with salsa mixture.

Each serving: About 235 calories, 14g protein, 20g carbohydrate, 11g total fat (4g saturated), 327mg cholesterol, 795mg sodium.

Tofu Stir-fry

We call for a bag of broccoli flowerets to save cutting and trimming time. Choose extrafirm tofu; other types will fall apart during stir-frying. To serve, spoon the saucy mixture over quick-cooking brown rice, another time-saver.

PREP: 25 MINUTES   COOK: 15 MINUTES
MAKES 4 MAIN-DISH SERVINGS.

3 tablespoons soy sauce
1 tablespoon brown sugar
1 tablespoon cornstarch
1 cup water
2 teaspoons vegetable oil
3 garlic cloves, crushed with garlic press
1 tablespoon peeled, grated fresh ginger
1/8 to 1/4 teaspoon crushed red pepper

1 bag (12 ounces) broccoli flowerets, cut into uniform pieces if necessary
8 ounces shiitake mushrooms, stems removed and caps thinly sliced
1 medium red pepper, cut into 1-inch pieces
1 package (15 ounces) extafirm tofu, patted dry and cut into 1-inch cubes
3 green onions, trimmed and thinly sliced

1. In small bowl, with wire whisk, mix soy sauce, brown sugar, cornstarch, and water until blended; set aside.

2. In deep nonstick 12-inch skillet, heat oil over medium-high heat until hot. Add garlic, ginger, and crushed red pepper and cook, stirring frequently (stir-frying), 30 seconds. Add broccoli, mushrooms, and red pepper and cook, covered, 8 minutes, stirring occasionally.

3. Add tofu and green onions and cook, uncovered, 2 minutes, stirring occasionally. Stir soy-sauce mixture to blend and add to skillet; heat to boiling. Boil, stirring, 1 minute.

Each serving: About 225 calories, 16g protein, 23g carbohydrate, 9g total fat (1g saturated), 0mg cholesterol, 775mg sodium.

Tofu Stir-fry

Ricotta-Spinach Calzone

Using refrigerated pizza-crust dough simplifies and shortens the preparation of these rich cheese and spinach–filled "pies."

PREP: 10 MINUTES   BAKE: 25 MINUTES
MAKES 4 MAIN-DISH SERVINGS.

1 cup part-skim ricotta cheese
1 cup shredded mozzarella cheese
  (4 ounces)
1 tablespoon cornstarch
1/2 teaspoon dried oregano
1 tube (10 ounces) refrigerated pizza-
  crust dough

1/2 cup marinara sauce
1 package (10 ounces) frozen
  chopped spinach, thawed and
  squeezed dry

1. Preheat oven to 400°F. In small bowl, combine ricotta, mozzarella, cornstarch, and oregano; stir until blended. Set aside.
2. Spray large cookie sheet with nonstick cooking spray. Unroll pizza dough in center of cookie sheet. With fingertips, press dough into 14" by 10" rectangle.
3. Spread cheese mixture lengthwise on half of dough, leaving 1-inch border. Spoon marinara sauce over cheese mixture; top with spinach. Fold other half of dough over filling. Pinch edges together to seal.
4. Bake calzone until well browned on top, 20 to 25 minutes. Cut calzone into 4 equal pieces to serve.

Each serving: About 400 calories, 21g protein, 43g carbohydrate, 15g total fat (5g saturated), 19mg cholesterol, 1,055mg sodium.

Pierogi and Sauerkraut-Slaw Casserole

This recipe couldn't be easier: just toss coleslaw mix with sauerkraut and seasonings, top with mini pierogi, then let the microwave do all the work!

PREP: 5 MINUTES   COOK: 12 MINUTES
MAKES 4 MAIN-DISH SERVINGS.

1 bag (16 ounces) shredded cabbage
  mix for coleslaw
1 bag (16 ounces) sauerkraut,
  drained
1/4 cup apple cider or apple juice
1/2 teaspoon caraway seeds

1/8 teaspoon ground black pepper
1 box (12 ounces) frozen mini pierogi
2 tablespoons chopped fresh dill
2 tablespoons butter or margarine,
  cut into pieces

1. In shallow 3-quart microwave-safe casserole, stir cabbage mix, sauerkraut, cider, caraway seeds, and pepper. In microwave oven, cook coleslaw mixture, covered, on High 5 minutes, stirring once halfway through cooking.

2. Arrange frozen pierogi over coleslaw mixture (it's OK if they overlap slightly). Sprinkle pierogi with dill and top with butter. Return casserole to microwave oven and cook, covered, on High until pierogi are hot, 5 to 7 minutes longer. Toss before serving.

Each serving: About 260 calories, 7g protein, 37g carbohydrate, 13g total fat (6g saturated), 65mg cholesterol, 837mg sodium.

Skillet Vegetable Curry

A package of precut cauliflower shortens prep time. As vegetables simmer, toast pita bread.

PREP: 15 MINUTES   COOK: 25 MINUTES

MAKES ABOUT 8 CUPS OR 4 MAIN-DISH SERVINGS.

3/4 pound cauliflower flowerets
1 large all-purpose potato (about
   8 ounces), peeled and cut into
   1-inch pieces
1 large sweet potato (about
   12 ounces), peeled and cut into
   1-inch pieces
2 tablespoons lightly packed
   sweetened flaked coconut
2 teaspoons olive oil
1 medium onion, finely chopped

1 teaspoon mustard seeds
1 1/2 teaspoons ground cumin
1 1/2 teaspoons ground coriander
1/8 teaspoon ground red pepper
   (cayenne)
2 medium tomatoes, chopped
1 cup frozen peas, thawed
1 1/4 teaspoons salt
1/2 cup loosely packed fresh
   cilantro leaves, chopped

1. In 4-quart saucepan, combine cauliflower, potato, sweet potato, and enough *water* to cover; heat to boiling over high heat. Reduce heat to low; cover and simmer until vegetables are tender, 8 to 10 minutes. Drain well, reserving 3/4 cup cooking water.

2. Meanwhile, in dry nonstick 12-inch skillet, cook coconut over medium heat, stirring constantly, until lightly browned, about 3 minutes; transfer to small bowl.

3. In same skillet, heat oil over medium heat until hot; add onion and cook 5 minutes. Add mustard seeds, cumin, coriander, and ground red pepper; cover and cook, shaking skillet frequently, until onion is tender and lightly browned and seeds start to pop, 5 minutes longer.

4. Spoon cauliflower mixture into skillet. Add tomatoes, peas, salt, and reserved cooking water; heat through. Sprinkle with cilantro to serve.

Each serving: About 230 calories, 8g protein, 43g carbohydrate, 4g total fat (1g saturated), 0mg cholesterol, 735mg sodium.

Barley-Vegetable Stew

A simple Italian gremolata of parsley, garlic, and lemon peel tops the stew to add a distinctive tangy element.

PREP: 10 MINUTES   COOK: 15 MINUTES
MAKES ABOUT 9 CUPS OR 4 MAIN-DISH SERVINGS.

1 cup quick-cooking barley
1 tablespoon olive oil
1 package (20 ounces) peeled butternut squash, cut into 1/2-inch pieces(4 cups)
2 medium stalks celery, cut into 1/2-inch pieces
1 medium onion, chopped
1 jar (14 to 16 ounces) marinara sauce

1 package (9 ounces) frozen cut green beans
1 cup vegetable broth
1/2 teaspoon salt
1/4 teaspoon ground black pepper
1/2 cup loosely packed fresh parsley leaves, chopped
1/2 teaspoon grated fresh lemon peel
1 small garlic clove, minced

1. Cook barley as label directs.

2. Meanwhile, in nonstick 12-inch skillet, heat oil over medium-high heat until hot. Add squash, celery, and onion; cover and cook, stirring occasionally, until lightly browned, about 10 minutes. Stir in marinara sauce, frozen beans, broth, salt, and pepper. Simmer, uncovered, 4 minutes, or until slightly thickened.

3. Meanwhile, in small bowl, with fork, mix parsley, lemon peel, and garlic; set aside.

4. Drain liquid, if any, from barley. Stir barley into vegetables. Sprinkle with parsley mixture to serve.

Each serving: About 320 calories, 9g protein, 60g carbohydrate, 7g total fat (1g saturated), 0mg cholesterol, 985mg sodium.

Vegetarian Phyllo Pizza

Delicate layers of phyllo form the crust of this rich, savory pizza.

PREP: 10 MINUTES BAKE: 15 MINUTES
MAKES 4 MAIN-DISH SERVINGS.

6 sheets (17" by 12" each) fresh or
frozen (thawed) phyllo
2 tablespoons butter or margarine,
melted
4 ounces soft, mild goat cheese such
as Montrâchet

1 jar (6 ounces) marinated artichoke
hearts, drained and cut into
1/4-inch pieces
1 1/2 cups grape or cherry tomatoes,
each cut in half

1. Preheat oven to 450°F. Place 1 sheet of phyllo on ungreased large cookie sheet; brush with some melted butter. Repeat layering with remaining phyllo and butter. Do not brush top layer.
2. Crumble goat cheese over phyllo; top with artichokes and tomatoes. Bake pizza until golden brown around the edges, 12 to 15 minutes.
3. Transfer pizza to large cutting board. With pizza cutter or knife, cut pizza lengthwise in half, then cut each half crosswise into 4 pieces.

Each serving: About 245 calories, 8g protein, 20g carbohydrate, 19g total fat (9g saturated), 29mg cholesterol, 387mg sodium.

Vegetarian Phyllo Pizza

Falafel Cones

Falafel is a staple of Middle Eastern cuisine. It is typically served as a snack or part of an appetizer plate.

PREP: 15 MINUTES COOK: 10 MINUTES
MAKES 4 MAIN-DISH SERVINGS.

2 cans (15 to 19 ounces each) low-sodium garbanzo beans, rinsed and well drained
2 garlic cloves, peeled
1 large egg
1 cup loosely packed fresh parsley leaves
1/4 cup tahini (sesame seed paste)
1 tablespoon dried mint leaves
2 teaspoons ground cumin

1/4 teaspoon ground red pepper (cayenne)
1/4 cup vegetable oil
2 plum tomatoes, chopped
1 green onion, trimmed and chopped
1 container (8 ounces) plain low-fat yogurt
1/4 teaspoon salt
4 pocketless pitas, warmed

1. In food processor, with knife blade attached, combine beans, garlic, egg, parsley, tahini, mint, cumin, and ground red pepper and puree until smooth. Shape mixture into sixteen 2-inch balls.

2. In nonstick 12-inch skillet, heat oil over medium-high heat until very hot but not smoking. Add falafel balls and cook, turning frequently, until evenly golden, 10 minutes.

3. Meanwhile, in small bowl, combine tomatoes, green onion, yogurt, and salt and stir until mixed.

4. To serve, shape each pita into a cone; tightly wrap bottom of each with kitchen parchment or foil to help hold its shape and prevent leakage. Fill each cone with 4 falafel balls and top with some yogurt mixture.

Each serving: About 670 calories, 28g protein, 94g carbohydrate, 22g total fat (4g saturated), 57mg cholesterol, 740mg sodium.

Vegetarian Tortilla Pie

Vegetarian Tortilla Pie

This dish can be assembled in a jiffy, thanks to its no-cook filling of canned black beans and corn, prepared salsa, and preshredded Jack cheese. A wedge of iceberg lettuce on the side with our Spicy Tomato Dressing (page 153) adds the missing crunch.

PREP: 8 MINUTES   BAKE: 12 MINUTES
MAKES 4 MAIN-DISH SERVINGS.

1 jar (11 to 12 ounces) medium salsa
1 can (8 ounces) no-salt-added
 tomato sauce
1 can (15 to 16 ounces) no-salt-
 added black beans, rinsed and
 drained
1 can (15 1/4 ounces) no-salt-added
 whole-kernel corn, drained

1/2 cup packed fresh cilantro leaves
4 (10-inch) low-fat flour tortillas
6 ounces shredded reduced-fat
 Monterey Jack cheese (1 1/2 cups)
reduced-fat sour cream (optional)

1. Preheat oven to 500°F. Spray 15 1/2" by 10 1/2" jelly-roll pan with nonstick cooking spray.
2. In small bowl, mix salsa and tomato sauce. In medium bowl, mix black beans, corn, and cilantro.
3. Place 1 tortilla in jelly-roll pan. Spread one-third of salsa mixture over tortilla. Top with one-third of bean mixture and one-third of cheese. Repeat layering 2 more times, ending with last tortilla.
4. Bake pie until cheese has melted and filling is hot, 10 to 12 minutes. Serve with reduced-fat sour cream, if you like.

Each serving without sour cream: Abut 440 calories, 25g protein, 65g carbohydrate, 11g total fat (5g saturated), 30mg cholesterol, 820mg sodium.

Queso-Blanco Soft Tacos

These tacos are filled with *queso blanco*, a white cheese that's a bit firmer than mozzarella, so it holds its shape when melted. Don't confuse it with *queso fresco*, a crumbly fresh cow's milk cheese that's found in almost every Latin American country.

PREP: 20 MINUTES   COOK: 5 MINUTES
MAKES 4 MAIN-DISH SERVINGS.

3 green onions, trimmed and thinly sliced

3 plum tomatoes, cut into 1/2-inch pieces

1 ripe avocado, peeled, pitted, and cut into 1/2-inch pieces

1/4 small head romaine lettuce, thinly sliced (2 cups)

1/4 cup loosely packed fresh cilantro leaves

1 cup mild or medium-hot salsa

1 package (12 ounces) queso blanco (Mexican frying cheese), cut into 12 slices

12 (6-inch) corn tortillas, warmed

1 lime, cut into 4 wedges

1. On platter, arrange green onions, tomatoes, avocado, lettuce, and cilantro. Pour salsa into serving bowl.

2. Heat nonstick 12-inch skillet over medium-high heat until hot. Add cheese and heat, turning once, until dark brown in spots, 2 to 3 minutes.

3. Place 1 cheese slice in each tortilla and fold in half. Serve tortillas immediately, adding green onions, tomatoes, avocado, lettuce, cilantro, salsa, and a squeeze of lime juice.

Each serving: About 545 calories, 26g protein, 49g carbohydrate, 29g total fat (13g saturated), 60mg cholesterol, 1,300mg sodium.

Queso-Blanco Soft Tacos

ONE-DISH MEALS

Gazpacho Style Pasta

s there a cook anywhere without a favorite one-dish meal in her or his repertoire? Maybe it's a comforting casserole you turn to when you're entertaining or an easy stir-fry on PTA night.

Whatever our favorites, most of us share a deep affection for one-dish meals—for good reason:

- Many can be prepared ahead of time.
- They free the cook from preparing time-consuming side dishes.
- Most require a minimum of prep time.
- They can be served from the vessel in which they were cooked, making cleanup a snap.

Those planning to add more meatless meals to their weekly menus will be delighted to know that in vegetarian cooking, one-dish meals are much more the norm than in traditional meat-based cooking.

So, gather the family for a cozy dinner of Lasagna Toss with Spinach and Ricotta or our Lentil Shepherd's Pie topped with mashed sweet potatoes laced with Indian spices. Both are served up right from the skillet. Having friends over for a casual dinner and a game of Scrabble? Savory Tomato Tart, layered with caramelized onions, goat cheese, and yellow and red tomatoes, is company-worthy. For an easy al fresco summer meal, fire up the coals for Grilled Tofu and Veggies, with a delightful gingery hoisin glaze. And when the leaves begin to fall, Mushroom and Barley Pilaf, with hearty root vegetables, will satisfy the need for stick-to-the-ribs comfort food.

This collection of one-dish meals includes almost fifty versatile, simple-to-fix recipes. From a classic Eggplant Parmesan to a fifteen-minute "fast-food" feast of Egg and Black Bean Burritos, you'll find dishes to please everyone at your table. There are creamy risottos, quick stir-fries, individual pizzas, pasta dishes aplenty, ethnic meals with authentic flair, pies and tarts that appeal to the eyes as well as to the palate.

As you work your way through these delectable recipes, don't be surprised to find that your repertoire of favorite one-dish meals has grown to include many of those on these pages.

New Mexico Green Chili

Variations on green chili are popular throughout New Mexico. This hearty vegetarian version is prepared with cannellini beans and vegetable broth. Tomatillos—a key ingredient—are small, green tomatolike fruits with papery husks. You can buy them fresh or canned. Serve with rice and top with a dollop of plain yogurt—delicious!

PREP: 1 HOUR   COOK: 40 MINUTES
MAKES ABOUT 8 1/2 CUPS OR 8 MAIN-DISH SERVINGS.

4 poblano chiles or 2 green peppers
1 tablespoon olive oil
1 large onion (12 ounces), cut into
 1/4-inch pieces
2 jalapeño chiles, seeded and minced
3 garlic cloves, crushed with garlic
 press
1/2 cup packed fresh cilantro leaves,
 chopped
1 teaspoon ground cumin

3/4 teaspoon salt
2 pounds tomatillos, husked, rinsed,
 and each cut into quarters or into
 eighths if large
1 can (14 1/2 ounces) vegetable broth
 (1 3/4 cups)
2 cans (15 to 19 ounces each) white
 kidney beans (cannellini), rinsed
 and drained

1. Preheat broiler. Line broiling pan with foil. Cut each pepper lengthwise in half; remove and discard stems and seeds. With hand, flatten each pepper half. Arrange peppers, cut side down, in prepared broiling pan. Place pan in broiler at closest position to heat source. Broil peppers until skin is charred and blistered, about 10 minutes. Wrap peppers with foil and allow to steam at room temperature until cool enough to handle, about 15 minutes. Remove peppers from foil. Peel off skin and discard. Cut peppers into 1-inch pieces.

2. In 6-quart Dutch oven, heat oil over medium heat until hot. Add onion, jalapeños, garlic, cilantro, cumin, and salt and cook 5 minutes.

3. Stir in tomatillos, broth, and roasted peppers; heat to boiling over high heat. Reduce heat to low; cover and simmer until tomatillos are tender, about 20 minutes. Stir in beans and cook until heated through, about 5 minutes longer.

Each serving: About 180 calories, 8g protein, 31g carbohydrate, 4g total fat (0g saturated), 0mg cholesterol, 605mg sodium.

Middle-Eastern Garbanzo Beans and Macaroni

A flavorful stew of pantry staples—canned beans and crushed tomatoes—tossed with pasta makes a satisfying vegetarian entrée.

PREP: 10 MINUTES   COOK: 35 MINUTES
MAKES ABOUT 8 CUPS OR 6 MAIN-DISH SERVINGS.

12 ounces macaroni twists or elbow
  macaroni
1 tablespoon olive oil
1 tablespoon butter or margarine
1 large onion (12 ounces), cut into
  1/4-inch pieces
2 garlic cloves, crushed with
  garlic press
1 teaspoon salt
1 teaspoon ground cumin

3/4 teaspoon ground coriander
1/4 teaspoon ground allspice
1/4 teaspoon coarsely ground
  black pepper
1 can (28 ounces) crushed tomatoes
1 can (15 to 19 ounces) garbanzo
  beans, rinsed and drained
1/4 cup loosely packed fresh parsley
  leaves, chopped
parsley sprigs for garnish

1. In large saucepot, cook pasta as label directs.

2. Meanwhile, in nonstick 12-inch skillet, heat oil with butter over medium heat until hot and melted. Add onion and cook, stirring occasionally, until tender and golden, about 20 minutes. Stir in garlic, salt, cumin, coriander, allspice, and pepper; cook 1 minute.

3. Add tomatoes and garbanzo beans to skillet; heat to boiling over medium-high heat. Reduce heat to medium-low; simmer, stirring occasionally, 5 minutes.

4. Drain pasta; return to saucepot. Toss garbanzo-bean mixture with pasta; heat through. Toss with chopped parsley just before serving. Garnish with parsley sprigs.

Each serving: About 400 calories, 14g protein, 73g carbohydrate, 7g total fat (2g saturated), 5mg cholesterol, 1,039mg sodium.

Middle-Eastern Garbanzo Beans and Macaroni

Lentil Shepherd's Pie

A steaming skillet of Indian-spiced lentils are topped with piping-hot curried mashed sweet potatoes for this nonmeat takeoff on an old comfort-food favorite.

PREP: 20 MINUTES   COOK: 35 MINUTES
MAKES 4 MAIN-DISH SERVINGS.

1 cup dry lentils, rinsed
1 tablespoon grated, peeled
  fresh ginger
1 teaspoon ground cumin
1 can (14 1/2 ounces) vegetable broth
  (1 3/4 cups)
1 bay leaf
2 cups water
1 tablespoon olive oil

1 teaspoon curry powder
1/8 teaspoon crushed red pepper
3 large sweet potatoes (about
  2 pounds), peeled and cut into
  1-inch pieces
1 teaspoon salt
2 green onions, trimmed and
  thinly sliced
plain yogurt (optional)

1. In 12-inch skillet, combine lentils, ginger, cumin, broth, bay leaf, and 1 1/4 cups water; heat to boiling over high heat. Reduce heat to medium; cover and cook until lentils are tender, about 20 minutes. Discard bay leaf.

2. Meanwhile, in 3-quart saucepan, heat oil over medium-high heat until hot. Add curry powder and red pepper and cook, stirring, 15 seconds; add sweet potatoes, salt, and remaining 3/4 cup water; heat to boiling. Reduce heat to medium-low; cover and cook, stirring occasionally, until potatoes are tender, about 15 minutes.

3. With potato masher or fork, mash potato mixture until almost smooth. Spoon mashed potatoes over lentil mixture in skillet; sprinkle with green onions. Serve with yogurt, if you like.

Each serving: About 410 calories, 18g protein, 77g carbohydrate, 5g total fat (1g saturated) 0mg cholesterol, 1,040mg sodium.

Microwave Tomato-Basil Risotto

You don't have to stand at the stove and stir, stir, stir to prepare this risotto—it's cooked in the microwave.

PREP: 5 MINUTES   COOK: 25 MINUTES
MAKES 4 MAIN-DISH SERVINGS.

3 1/2 cups vegetable broth
1/2 cup dry white wine
3/4 cup loosely packed fresh
   basil leaves
1 tablespoon olive oil
1 medium shallot, minced
2 cups Arborio rice (Italian short-
   grain rice) or medium-grain rice

3 medium tomatoes (8 ounces each)
3/4 teaspoon salt
1/4 teaspoon coarsely ground
   black pepper
1/2 cup freshly grated Parmesan
   cheese

1. In covered 2-quart saucepan, heat broth and wine over high heat until bubbles form around edge of pan. Meanwhile, coarsely chop basil.

2. In 3 1/2- to 4-quart microwave-safe casserole or bowl, combine oil, shallot, and 1/4 cup chopped basil. Cook, uncovered, in microwave oven on High until shallot has softened, about 1 minute. Add rice and stir until rice grains are opaque. Cook on High 1 minute.

3. Stir hot broth into rice in casserole. Cover and cook on Medium (50% power), stirring once, until most of liquid has been absorbed, about 15 minutes. Meanwhile, chop tomatoes.

4. Stir tomatoes, salt, and pepper into rice mixture. Cover and cook on High, stirring once, until rice is tender but still firm, 3 to 4 minutes. Stir in Parmesan and remaining chopped basil.

Each serving: About 550 calories, 15g protein, 97g carbohydrate, 8g total fat (3g saturated), 8mg cholesterol, 1,490mg sodium.

Editor's Note

This recipe was tested in an 1,100-watt microwave oven. If your microwave has more or less power, it may be necessary to adjust the cooking time.

Classic Risotto

These meatless main courses are great with a generous mixed green salad.

PREP: 10 MINUTES   COOK: 40 MINUTES
MAKES ABOUT 5 1/2 CUPS OR 4 MAIN-DISH SERVINGS.

1 tablespoon butter or margarine
1 medium onion, finely chopped
1 can (14 1/2 ounces) vegetable broth
   (1 3/4 cups)
3 1/2 cups water
2 cups Arborio rice (Italian short-
   grain rice) or medium-grain rice

1/2 teaspoon salt
1/4 teaspoon coarsely ground black
   pepper
1/2 cup dry white wine
1/2 cup freshly grated Parmesan
   cheese

1. In 4 1/2- to 5-quart saucepot or Dutch oven, melt butter over medium heat. Add onion and cook, stirring occasionally, until tender, about 10 minutes.

2. Meanwhile, in 2-quart saucepan, heat broth and water to boiling over high heat. Reduce heat to low to maintain simmer; cover.

3. Add rice, salt, and pepper to onion and cook, stirring frequently, until rice grains are opaque, 2 to 3 minutes. Increase heat to medium-high; add wine and cook, stirring, until wine has been absorbed.

4. Add 1/2 cup simmering broth mixture to rice, stirring until liquid has been absorbed. Continue cooking, adding broth 1/2 cup at a time and stirring after each addition, until all liquid has been absorbed and rice is tender but still firm, about 20 minutes longer (risotto should have a creamy consistency). Remove risotto from heat; stir in Parmesan.

Each serving: About 345 calories, 9g protein, 63g carbohydrate, 4g total fat (3g saturated), 13mg cholesterol, 621mg sodium.

Lemon Risotto: From *1 lemon*, grate 2 tablespoons peel and squeeze 1 tablespoon juice. Prepare Classic Risotto, but stir in lemon peel and juice with Parmesan in step 4. Makes about 5 ½ cups or 4 main-dish servings.

Each serving: About 345 calories, 9g protein, 65g carbohydrate, 4g total fat (3g saturated), 13mg cholesterol, 621mg sodium.

Mixed Mushroom Risotto: In nonstick 10-inch skillet, melt *1 tablespoon butter* over medium-high heat. Add *three 4-ounce packages mixed sliced mushrooms* and cook, stirring, until tender and golden, about 10 minutes; set aside. Prepare Classic Risotto, but stir in mushroom mixture with Parmesan in step 4; heat through. Makes about 6 cups or 4 main-dish servings.

Each serving: About 565 calories, 15g protein, 99g carbohydrate, 10g total fat (4g saturated), 16mg cholesterol, 976mg sodium.

Carrot Risotto

Carrot Risotto

This quick microwave risotto gets its lovely color and great flavor from shredded carrots and carrot juice.

PREP: 10 MINUTES   COOK: 25 MINUTES
MAKES ABOUT 6 CUPS OR 4 MAIN-DISH SERVINGS.

1 can or bottle (12 to 15 ounces) carrot juice plus enough water to equal 2 cups
1 can (14 1/2 ounces) vegetable broth (1 3/4 cups)
1/2 cup dry white wine
1 1/4 cups water
1 tablespoon olive oil
2 cups shredded carrots

1/2 small onion, finely chopped
2 cups Arborio rice (Italian short-grain rice) or medium-grain rice
1/3 cup freshly grated Parmesan cheese
3/4 teaspoon salt
1/4 teaspoon ground black pepper
2 tablespoons coarsely chopped fresh mint or parsley (optional)

1. In 2-quart saucepan, heat carrot juice, broth, wine, and water to boiling over high heat. Reduce heat to low to maintain simmer; cover.

2. In 3- to 3 1/2-quart microwave-safe casserole, combine oil, carrots, and onion. Cook, uncovered, in microwave oven on High until onion has softened, about 2 minutes. Add rice and stir until rice grains are opaque. Cook on High 1 minute.

3. Stir hot liquid into rice mixture. Cover casserole with lid or vented plastic wrap and cook on Medium (50% power) until most of liquid has been absorbed and rice is tender but still firm, 15 to 20 minutes. Stir in Parmesan, salt, and pepper. Sprinkle with mint, if you like.

Each serving: About 570 calories, 15g protein, 105g carbohydrate, 7g total fat (2g saturated), 7mg cholesterol, 1,110mg sodium.

Asparagus Risotto

Sweet asparagus lends fresh spring flavor to this favorite Italian rice dish.

PREP: 15 MINUTES   COOK: 50 MINUTES
MAKES ABOUT 8 CUPS OR 4 MAIN-DISH SERVINGS.

1 can (14 1/2 ounces) vegetable broth (1 3/4 cups)
4 cups water
1 1/2 pounds asparagus, trimmed
2 tablespoons butter or margarine
1 small onion, finely chopped
2 cups Arborio rice (Italian short-grain rice) or medium-grain rice

1/2 cup dry white wine
3/4 cup freshly grated Parmesan cheese
3/4 teaspoon salt
1/4 teaspoon ground black pepper

1. In 2-quart saucepan, heat broth and water to boiling over high heat. Reduce heat to low to maintain simmer; cover.

2. If using thin asparagus, cut each stalk crosswise in half and reserve halves with tips; if using medium asparagus, cut 1 inch from asparagus tops and reserve tips. Cut remaining asparagus stalks into 1/4-inch pieces.

3. In deep nonstick 12-inch skillet, melt 1 tablespoon of the butter over medium heat. Add onion and asparagus pieces (not tips) and cook, stirring occasionally, until vegetables begin to soften, about 10 minutes.

4. Add rice and the remaining 1 tablespoon butter and cook, stirring frequently, until rice grains are opaque. Increase heat to medium-high; add wine and cook, stirring, until wine has been absorbed.

5. Add 1/2 cup simmering broth to rice, stirring until liquid has been absorbed. Continue cooking, adding broth 1/2 cup at a time and stirring after each addition, until all liquid has been absorbed, about 25 minutes. Stir in reserved asparagus when adding last 1/2 cup broth and cook until all liquid has been absorbed and rice and asparagus are tender (risotto should have a creamy consistency). Stir in Parmesan, salt, and pepper.

Each serving: About 590 calories, 19g protein, 96g carbohydrate, 14g total fat (7g saturated), 28mg cholesterol, 1,227mg sodium.

Couscous Tabbouleh

Instead of the traditional bulgur wheat, this quick tabbouleh is made with couscous. Garbanzo beans add extra protein.

PREP: 20 MINUTES
MAKES 4 MAIN-DISH SERVINGS.

3/4 cup water
3/4 cup couscous
3/4 teaspoon salt
1 can (15 to 19 ounces) garbanzo beans, drained and rinsed
4 medium tomatoes (about 1 1/4 pounds), cut into 1/2-inch pieces
2 Kirby (pickling) cucumbers (about 4 ounces each), unpeeled and cut into 1/2-inch pieces

3/4 cup loosely packed fresh flat-leaf parsley leaves, chopped
1/2 cup loosely packed fresh mint leaves, chopped
1/4 cup fresh lemon juice (from about 2 lemons)
2 tablespoons olive oil
1/4 teaspoon coarsely ground black pepper

1. In microwave-safe 3-quart bowl, heat water to boiling in microwave oven on High, 1 1/2 to 2 minutes. Remove bowl from microwave. Stir in couscous and 1/4 teaspoon salt; cover and let stand until liquid has been absorbed, about 5 minutes.

2. Fluff couscous with fork. Stir in beans, tomatoes, cucumbers, parsley, mint, lemon juice, oil, pepper, and remaining 1/2 teaspoon salt. Serve couscous at room temperature or cover and refrigerate up to 6 hours.

Each serving: About 350 calories, 13g protein, 56g carbohydrate, 9g total fat (1g saturated), 0mg cholesterol, 700mg sodium.

Spaghetti Primavera

A vegetable medley of asparagus, broccoli, and carrots tossed with spaghetti, fresh basil, and Parmesan.

PREP: 20 MINUTES   COOK: 30 MINUTES
MAKES 4 MAIN-DISH SERVINGS.

4 tablespoons butter or margarine
3 medium carrots, cut lengthwise
  into matchstick-thin strips
1 medium onion, chopped
2 garlic cloves, crushed with
  garlic press
salt
1 package (16 ounces) spaghetti
1 bag (16 ounces) broccoli flowerets
1 pound asparagus, trimmed and cut
  diagonally into 1-inch pieces

3/4 teaspoon salt
1/8 to 1/4 teaspoon crushed
  red pepper
1/2 cup water
1 cup loosely packed fresh basil
  leaves, chopped
1/2 cup freshly grated Parmesan
  cheese

1. In nonstick 12-inch skillet, melt 2 tablespoons butter over medium heat. Add carrots and onion and cook, stirring occasionally, until tender and golden, about 10 minutes. Add garlic; cook, stirring, 1 minute.

2. Meanwhile, in large saucepot cook pasta as label directs.

3. To carrot mixture in skillet, add broccoli, asparagus, salt, crushed red pepper, and water; heat to boiling over medium-high heat. Reduce heat to medium; cover and cook, stirring occasionally, until vegetables are tender, 6 to 10 minutes longer.

4. Drain pasta, reserving 3/4 cup pasta water; return pasta to saucepot. Add basil, Parmesan, remaining 2 tablespoons butter, and reserved pasta water; toss well. Add vegetable mixture and gently toss to combine.

Each serving: About 655 calories, 25g protein, 101g carbohydrate, 22g total fat (9g saturated), 39mg cholesterol, 946mg sodium.

Triple-Mushroom Fettuccine

The rich, earthy flavors of shiitake, cremini, and oyster mushrooms are combined with hearty fettuccine noodles to make a satisfying and easy family dish that's special enough for company.

PREP: 20 MINUTES   COOK: 25 MINUTES
MAKES 4 MAIN-DISH SERVINGS.

1 package (16 ounces) fettuccine or linguine
2 tablespoons butter or margarine
1 medium onion, finely chopped
3 packages (4 ounces each) sliced wild mushroom blend or 1 pound mixed wild mushrooms, stems discarded and caps thinly sliced
2 garlic cloves, crushed with garlic press

1/4 teaspoon dried thyme
1/2 teaspoon salt
1/4 teaspoon coarsely ground black pepper
1 can (14 1/2 ounces) reduced-sodium vegetable broth (1 3/4 cups)
1 cup loosely packed fresh parsley leaves, chopped

1. In large saucepot, cook pasta as label directs.

2. Meanwhile, in nonstick 12-inch skillet, melt butter over medium heat. Add onion and cook, stirring occasionally, until tender, 8 to 10 minutes. Increase heat to medium-high. Add mushrooms, garlic, thyme, salt, and pepper and cook, stirring often, until mushrooms are golden and liquid has evaporated, 10 minutes.

3. Add broth to mushroom mixture and heat to boiling, stirring occasionally.

4. Drain pasta; return to saucepot. Add mushroom mixture and parsley; toss well.

Each serving: About 530 calories, 19g protein, 95g carbohydrate, 11g total fat (4g saturated), 16mg cholesterol, 762mg sodium.

Quick-Comfort Egg Noodles and Cabbage

Old-fashioned curly egg noodles are combined with caramelized onion, cabbage, and peas for a cozy family dinner.

PREP: 15 MINUTES   COOK: 30 MINUTES
MAKES 4 MAIN-DISH SERVINGS.

1 package (12 ounces) curly wide
  egg noodles
1 tablespoon butter or margarine
1 tablespoon olive oil
1 jumbo onion (1 pound), thinly sliced
1 small head (about 1 1/4 pounds)
  savoy cabbage, thinly sliced,
  with tough ribs discarded
1 teaspoon fresh thyme leaves or
  1/4 teaspoon dried thyme

3/4 teaspoon salt
1/4 teaspoon coarsely ground
  black pepper
1 package (10 ounces) frozen peas
1 cup vegetable broth
1/4 cup freshly grated Parmesan
  cheese
thyme sprigs for garnish

1. In large saucepot, cook pasta as label directs.
2. Meanwhile, in nonstick 12-inch skillet, heat butter and oil over medium heat until melted and hot. Add onion and cook, stirring occasionally, until onion is tender and golden, about 20 minutes. Increase heat to medium-high; add cabbage, thyme, salt, and pepper and cook, stirring occasionally, until cabbage is tender-crisp and golden, 5 minutes. Stir in frozen peas and broth; cook, stirring, 2 minutes.
3. Drain noodles; return to saucepot. Add cabbage mixture and Parmesan; toss well. Garnish with thyme sprigs.

Each serving: About 540 calories, 22g protein, 88g carbohydrate, 13g total fat (4g saturated), 93mg cholesterol, 1,041mg sodium.

Quick-Comfort Egg Noodles and Cabbage

Lasagna Toss with Spinach and Ricotta

Lasagna Toss with Spinach and Ricotta

This recipe has all the flavor of a layered and baked lasagna, without the wait! Lasagna noodles are tossed with a speedy tomato-spinach skillet sauce, then dolloped with ricotta cheese to serve.

PREP: 20 MINUTES   COOK: 35 MINUTES

MAKES 4 MAIN-DISH SERVINGS.

1 package (16 ounces) lasagna noodles
1 tablespoon olive oil
1 medium onion, finely chopped
2 garlic cloves, crushed with garlic press
1 can (28 ounces) plum tomatoes
3/4 teaspoon salt
1/4 teaspoon coarsely ground black pepper

1 package (10 ounces) frozen chopped spinach
1/2 cup loosely packed fresh basil leaves, chopped
1/4 cup freshly grated Parmesan cheese, plus additional for serving (optional)
1 cup part-skim ricotta cheese

1. In large saucepot, cook lasagna noodles as label directs, increasing cooking time to 12 to 14 minutes.

2. Meanwhile, in nonstick 12-inch skillet, heat oil over medium heat until hot. Add onion and cook, stirring occasionally, until tender, about 10 minutes. Add garlic and cook, stirring, 30 seconds.

3. Stir in tomatoes with their juice, salt, and pepper, breaking up tomatoes with side of spoon; heat to boiling over high heat. Reduce heat to medium and cook, uncovered, 8 minutes. Add frozen spinach and cook, covered, until spinach is tender, about 10 minutes, stirring occasionally. Stir in basil.

4. Drain noodles; return to saucepot. Add tomato mixture and Parmesan; toss well. Spoon into 4 pasta bowls; top with dollops of ricotta cheese. Serve with additional Parmesan, if you like.

Each serving: About 620 calories, 28g protein, 100g carbohydrate, 12g total fat (5g saturated), 23mg cholesterol, 1,640mg sodium.

Fettuccine with Fresh Herbs and Tomatoes

Toss fettuccine with basil, mint, sage, rosemary, and tomatoes, and sprinkle with ricotta salata cheese.

PREP: 15 MINUTES   COOK: 15 MINUTES
MAKES 4 MAIN-DISH SERVINGS.

1 package (16 ounces) fettuccine or linguine

1 cup loosely packed fresh basil leaves, chopped

3/4 cup loosely packed fresh mint leaves, chopped

2 tablespoons fresh rosemary leaves, chopped

1 tablespoon fresh sage leaves, chopped

2 large tomatoes (about 8 ounces each), chopped

2 tablespoons extravirgin olive oil

3/4 teaspoon salt

1/4 teaspoon ground black pepper

1/2 cup crumbled ricotta salata or 1/4 cup freshly grated Parmesan cheese

1. In large saucepot, cook pasta as label directs.

2. Meanwhile, in large serving bowl, toss basil, mint, rosemary, sage, tomatoes, oil, salt, and pepper; set aside.

3. Drain pasta, reserving 1/2 cup pasta water. Add pasta and reserved pasta water to herb mixture; toss well. Sprinkle with cheese to serve.

Each serving: About 565 calories, 19g protein, 93g carbohydrate, 13g total fat (4g saturated), 17mg cholesterol, 920mg sodium.

Roasted Vegetables with Arugula and Whole-Wheat Fusilli

Roasted butternut squash, peppers, and onions are tossed with fresh arugula leaves, whole-wheat pasta, and a splash of vinegar. If you can't find precut butternut squash at your grocery store, buy one that weighs 2 pounds and peel, seed, and cut it up yourself.

PREP: 25 MINUTES   ROAST: 50 MINUTES
MAKES 4 MAIN-DISH SERVINGS.

1 package (about 20 ounces) peeled and precut butternut squash, cut into 1-inch pieces
4 garlic cloves, each cut in half
2 medium red onions, each cut into 8 wedges
2 medium red peppers, cut into 1/2-inch-wide strips
2 tablespoons olive oil
1 teaspoon salt
1/4 teaspoon coarsely ground black pepper

1 pound whole-wheat fusilli or corkscrew pasta
2 bunches arugula (about 4 ounces each), trimmed and coarsely chopped
2 tablespoons white or dark balsamic vinegar
freshly grated Parmesan cheese (optional)

1. Preheat oven to 450°F. In 15 1/2" by 10 1/2" jelly-roll pan, toss squash, garlic, onions, red peppers, oil, salt, and pepper until evenly mixed. Roast, stirring occasionally, until vegetables are tender and lightly golden, about 50 minutes.

2. Meanwhile, in large saucepot, cook pasta as label directs.

3. Drain pasta, reserving 1/2 cup pasta water; return pasta to saucepot. Add roasted vegetables, arugula, vinegar, and reserved pasta water; toss until well mixed. Serve with Parmesan, if you like.

Each serving: About 610 calories, 19g protein, 115g carbohydrate, 9g total fat (1g saturated), 0mg cholesterol, 610mg sodium.

Fusilli with No-Cook Tomato Sauce

It's our quickest trick: Combine ripe tomatoes with fragrant basil and zesty olives for a satisfying sauce that goes well with any pasta.

PREP: 10 MINUTES   COOK: 15 MINUTES
MAKES 4 MAIN-DISH SERVINGS.

1 package (16 ounces) long fusilli pasta
2 pounds ripe tomatoes (about 6 medium), cut into 1/2-inch pieces
1 cup packed fresh basil leaves, coarsely chopped

1/2 cup pimiento-stuffed olives, chopped, or salad olives
2 tablespoons olive oil
1 tablespoon red wine vinegar
1 teaspoon salt
1/4 teaspoon ground black pepper

1. In large saucepot, cook pasta as label directs. Drain.
2. Meanwhile, in large serving bowl, combine tomatoes (with their juice), basil, olives, oil, vinegar, salt, and pepper; stir gently to mix well.
3. Toss pasta with tomato sauce.

Each serving: About 550 calories, 17g protein, 96g carbohydrate, 11g total fat (2g saturated), 0mg cholesterol, 1,065mg sodium.

Rotelle with Ratatouille

Roasting the eggplant, pepper, and onion for this dish may take a little longer than top-of-the-range cooking, but it's low-maintenance and the resulting rich flavor is worth it.

PREP: 20 MINUTES   ROAST: 40 MINUTES
MAKES 4 MAIN-DISH SERVINGS.

1 medium eggplant (about 1½ pounds), cut into 1-inch pieces
1 medium red pepper, cut into 1-inch pieces
1 large red onion, cut into 1-inch pieces
2 garlic cloves, crushed with garlic press
3 tablespoons olive oil
1½ teaspoons salt

½ teaspoon ground black pepper
1 pint red and/or yellow cherry tomatoes, each cut in half
1 cup loosely packed fresh basil leaves, coarsely chopped
1 tablespoon red wine vinegar
1 package (16 ounces) rotelle or fusilli pasta
fresh basil leaves for garnish

1. Preheat oven to 450°F. In large roasting pan (17" by 11½") or 15½" by 10½" jelly-roll pan, toss eggplant, red pepper, onion, garlic, oil, salt, and pepper until vegetables are well coated. Roast, stirring occasionally, until vegetables are tender and lightly browned, 35 to 40 minutes.

2. In large bowl, toss tomatoes, chopped basil, and vinegar; set aside to allow flavors to develop.

3. Meanwhile, in large saucepot, cook pasta as label directs. Drain pasta, reserving ¼ cup pasta water.

4. Add pasta, roasted vegetables, and reserved pasta water to tomatoes in bowl; toss well. Garnish each serving with basil leaves.

Each serving: About 595 calories, 18g protein, 104g carbohydrate, 13g total fat (2g saturated), 0mg cholesterol, 1,040mg sodium.

Bow Ties with Butternut Squash and Peas

This vegetarian main dish of pasta tossed with butternut squash, peas, and a creamy Parmesan sauce makes a great family dinner. For a low-fat version, use fat-free half-and-half.

PREP: 20 MINUTES   COOK: 15 MINUTES
MAKES 6 MAIN-DISH SERVINGS.

1 package (16 ounces) bow-tie or corkscrew pasta
1 medium butternut squash (2 1/4 pounds), peeled, seeded, and cut into 1-inch pieces
1 package (10 ounces) frozen peas
3/4 cup half-and-half or light cream
1 teaspoon minced fresh sage leaves
1/3 cup freshly grated Parmesan cheese
1 teaspoon salt
1/4 teaspoon coarsely ground black pepper

1. In large saucepot, cook pasta as label directs. Drain.
2. Meanwhile, place squash chunks in 2 1/2-quart microwave-safe baking dish; cover and cook in microwave oven on High, stirring once, 12 minutes. Stir in peas, half-and-half, and sage and cook, uncovered, 2 minutes.
3. In large warm serving bowl, toss pasta with squash mixture, Parmesan, salt, and pepper.

Each serving: About 430 calories, 16g protein, 78g carbohydrate, 7g total fat (3g saturated), 15mg cholesterol, 650mg sodium.

Bow Ties with Butternut Squash and Peas

Gazpacho-Style Pasta

Gazpacho-Style Pasta

Classic gazpacho soup ingredients get pulsed in the food processor while the small seashell pasta cooks. Serve with soup spoons!

PREP: 15 MINUTES   COOK: 15 MINUTES
MAKES 4 MAIN-DISH SERVINGS.

1 package (16 ounces) small shell or orecchiette pasta
1 English (seedless) cucumber (about 1 pound), unpeeled and cut into 2-inch pieces
1/2 medium yellow pepper, cut into 1-inch pieces
1/2 medium red pepper, cut into 1-inch pieces
1/2 medium red onion, cut into 1-inch pieces
1 jalapeño chile, seeded and cut into 1/2-inch pieces

1 garlic clove, cut into thirds
1 1/2 pounds tomatoes (about 5 medium), cut into 1/2-inch pieces
2 tablespoons olive oil
2 tablespoons sherry or red wine vinegar
1 1/2 teaspoons salt
1 small bunch fresh parsley, stems discarded
cucumber slices and cherry tomatoes for garnish

1. In large saucepot, cook pasta as label directs. Drain.

2. Meanwhile, in food processor, with knife blade attached, finely chop cucumber, peppers, onion, chile, and garlic. Do *not* puree.

3. In large serving bowl, toss vegetable mixture with tomatoes, oil, vinegar, and salt until well mixed. Set aside 4 parsley leaves for garnish; chop remaining parsley.

4. Add pasta and chopped parsley to vegetable mixture; toss well to combine. Garnish each serving with cucumber slices, cherry tomatoes, and reserved parsley leaves.

Each serving: About 555 calories, 18g protein, 100g carbohydrate, 9g total fat (1g saturated), 0mg cholesterol, 1,045mg sodium.

Trattoria-Style Pasta and Beans

A dish the entire family will be asking for! A comforting mixture of vegetables, pasta, and beans is cooked in a flavorful tomato broth. Serve with a mixed green salad to round out the meal.

PREP: 15 MINUTES   COOK: 40 MINUTES

MAKES ABOUT 8 CUPS OR 4 MAIN-DISH SERVINGS.

1 cup tubetti or ditalini pasta
1 tablespoon olive oil
1 medium onion, finely chopped
1 carrot, peeled and finely chopped
1 stalk celery, finely chopped
1 garlic clove, minced
1 can (15$^{1}/_{2}$ to 19 ounces) no-salt-added white kidney beans (cannellini), rinsed and drained

1 can (14$^{1}/_{2}$ ounces) diced tomatoes
$^{1}/_{2}$ teaspoon salt
$^{1}/_{4}$ teaspoon coarsely ground black pepper
4 cups water
$^{1}/_{4}$ cup freshly grated Parmesan cheese
$^{1}/_{4}$ cup loosely packed fresh parsley leaves, chopped

1. In 3-quart saucepan, cook pasta as label directs. Drain.

2. Meanwhile, in 4-quart saucepan, heat oil over medium heat until hot. Add onion, carrot, and celery and cook, stirring occasionally, until vegetables are tender, about 15 minutes. Add garlic and cook, stirring, 1 minute.

3. Add beans, tomatoes, salt, pepper, and water; heat to boiling over high heat. Reduce heat to medium-low and simmer, uncovered, 20 minutes.

4. Add pasta, Parmesan, and parsley to vegetable mixture; heat through.

Each serving: About 295 calories, 14g protein, 48g carbohydrate, 6g total fat (2g saturated), 4mg cholesterol, 865mg sodium.

Pasta with Broccoli Rabe and Garbanzos

A classic combination of bitter greens and sweet golden raisins tossed with pasta and beans for a quick meal.

PREP: 20 MINUTES   COOK: 20 MINUTES
MAKES 4 MAIN-DISH SERVINGS.

1 package (16 ounces) penne or ziti pasta
2 bunches broccoli rabe (about 12 ounces each), tough stems trimmed
2 tablespoons olive oil
3 garlic cloves, crushed with side of chef's knife
1/4 teaspoon crushed red pepper
1 can (15 to 19 ounces) garbanzo beans, rinsed and drained
1/4 cup golden raisins
1 1/4 teaspoons salt
freshly grated Parmesan cheese (optional)

1. In large saucepot, cook pasta as label directs.
2. Meanwhile, in another large saucepot, heat *4 quarts water* to boiling. Add broccoli rabe and cook until thickest parts of stems are tender, 3 to 5 minutes. Drain broccoli rabe; cool slightly. Cut broccoli rabe into 2-inch pieces.
3. Wipe saucepot dry. Add oil and heat over medium-high heat until hot. Add garlic and crushed red pepper and cook, stirring, 1 minute. Add broccoli rabe, garbanzo beans, and raisins; cook, stirring frequently, until heated through, about 3 minutes. Remove saucepot from heat.
4. Drain pasta, reserving 2/3 cup pasta cooking water. Add pasta, reserved pasta water, and salt to broccoli rabe mixture; toss well. Serve with Parmesan, if you like.

Each serving: About 665 calories, 25g protein, 119g carbohydrate, 11g total fat (1g saturated), 0mg cholesterol, 1,160mg sodium.

Pasta with No-Cook Tomato and Bocconcini Sauce

Bocconcini (Italian for "little mouthfuls") are small balls of mozzarella that can be found packed in whey or water in gourmet shops and in the dairy case of some supermarkets. Sometimes they have been tossed with herbs such as basil and black and crushed red pepper. In this case adjust the seasonings that are called for accordingly.

PREP: 20 MINUTES PLUS STANDING   COOK: 15 MINUTES
MAKES 6 MAIN-DISH SERVINGS.

- 2 pints cherry tomatoes, each cut in half
- 1/2 cup loosely packed fresh flat-leaf parsley leaves, chopped
- 1/2 cup loosely packed fresh basil leaves, thinly sliced
- 1/4 cup olive oil
- 1 teaspoon salt
- 1/4 teaspoon coarsely ground black pepper
- 1 garlic clove, crushed with garlic press
- 1 package (16 ounces) penne or corkscrew pasta
- 12 ounces small mozzarella balls (bocconcini), each cut in half

1. In large serving bowl, stir cherry tomatoes, parsley, basil, oil, salt, pepper, and garlic. Let stand at room temperature at least 1 hour or up to 4 hours to blend flavors.
2. In large saucepot, cook pasta as label directs. Drain well.
3. Add pasta to tomato mixture; toss with bocconcini.

Each serving: About 545 calories, 21g protein, 64g carbohydrate, 23g total fat (9g saturated), 44mg cholesterol, 540mg sodium.

Pasta with No-Cook Tomato and Bocconcini Sauce

Pasta Puttanesca with Arugula

For a refreshing summer meal, mix pasta with a perky caper and shallot dressing and lots of cut-up fresh tomatoes, chopped arugula, and basil.

PREP: 15 MINUTES   COOK: 15 MINUTES
MAKES 4 MAIN-DISH SERVINGS.

1 package (16 ounces) gemelli or
  corkscrew pasta
1 1/2 pounds tomatoes (about 5
  medium), cut into 1/2-inch pieces
1 medium shallot, minced (about
  1/4 cup)
1 garlic clove, crushed with garlic
  press
2 tablespoons olive oil
2 tablespoons capers, drained and
  chopped

1 tablespoon red wine vinegar
1/2 teaspoon grated fresh lemon peel
1/4 teaspoon crushed red pepper
2 bunches arugula (about 4 ounces
  each), tough stems removed,
  leaves coarsely chopped
1 cup packed fresh basil leaves,
  chopped

1. In large saucepot, cook pasta as label directs. Drain.
2. Meanwhile, in large serving bowl, toss tomatoes with shallot, garlic, oil, capers, vinegar, lemon peel, and crushed red pepper until well mixed.
3. Add pasta to tomato mixture and toss to combine. Just before serving, gently toss warm pasta mixture with arugula and basil until greens are slightly wilted.

Each serving: About 540 calories, 18g protein, 97g carbohydrate, 10g total fat (1g saturated), 0mg cholesterol, 310mg sodium.

Macaroni and Cheese on the Light Side

Our pasta recipe is amazingly creamy, and it sneaks vegetables into the kids' dinner without a lot of fuss.

PREP: 20 MINUTES   COOK: 20 MINUTES
MAKES 8 MAIN-DISH SERVINGS.

1 package (16 ounces) cavatelli
   pasta
2 tablespoons butter or margarine
3 tablespoons all-purpose flour
1/2 teaspoon salt
1/4 teaspoon ground black pepper
pinch ground nutmeg

3 1/2 cups low-fat milk (1%)
6 ounces (1 1/2 cups) reduced-fat
   sharp Cheddar cheese, shredded
1/3 cup grated Parmesan cheese
1 package (10 ounces) frozen mixed
   vegetables

1. In large saucepot, cook pasta as label directs.

2. Meanwhile, in 3-quart nonreactive saucepan, melt butter over medium heat. With wire whisk, stir in flour, salt, pepper, and nutmeg; cook, stirring constantly, 1 minute. Gradually whisk in milk and cook over medium-high heat, stirring constantly, until sauce boils and thickens slightly. Boil, stirring, 1 minute.

3. Remove saucepan from heat; stir in Cheddar and Parmesan just until melted. Following manufacturer's instructions, use immersion blender to blend mixture in saucepan until smooth. (Or, in blender at low speed, with center part of cover removed to let steam escape, puree sauce mixture in small batches until smooth. Pour the sauce into bowl after each batch.)

4. Place frozen vegetables in colander; drain pasta over vegetables. Return pasta and vegetables to saucepot; stir in cheese sauce.

Each serving: About 340 calories, 18g protein, 43g carbohydrate, 12g total fat (5g saturated), 40mg cholesterol, 576mg sodium.

Lo Mein with Tofu, Snow Peas, and Carrots

Lo Mein with Tofu, Snow Peas, and Carrots

Lo mein is a Chinese dish of boiled noodles that are stir-fried with any number of vegetables and tofu or other protein and tossed with a soy-based sauce. We've sped up the process with ramen and stir-fry sauce.

PREP: 15 MINUTES   COOK: 15 MINUTES
MAKES 4 MAIN-DISH SERVINGS.

2 packages (3 ounces each) Oriental-flavor ramen noodle soup mix
2 teaspoons vegetable oil
1 package (14 to 15 ounces) extrafirm tofu, patted dry and cut into 1/2-inch cubes
6 ounces snow peas, strings removed and each cut diagonally in half (about 2 cups)

3 green onions, trimmed and cut into 2-inch pieces
1 1/2 cups shredded carrots
1/2 cup bottled stir-fry sauce
3 ounces fresh bean sprouts (about 1 cup), rinsed and drained

1. In 4-quart saucepan, cook ramen noodles (reserve flavor packets) 2 minutes. Drain noodles, reserving 1/4 cup noodle water.

2. Meanwhile, in nonstick 12-inch skillet, heat oil over medium-high heat until very hot. Add tofu and cook, stirring occasionally, until lightly browned, 5 to 6 minutes. Add snow peas and green onions; cook, stirring frequently (stir-frying), until vegetables are tender-crisp, 3 to 5 minutes. Stir in the carrots, stir-fry sauce, and contents of 1 flavor packet to taste (depending on salt level of sauce) and cook until carrots are tender, about 2 minutes. (Discard remaining flavor packet or reserve for another use.)

3. Reserve some bean sprouts for garnish. Add noodles, reserved noodle water, and remaining bean sprouts to skillet; cook, stirring, 1 minute to blend flavors. Sprinkle with reserved bean sprouts to serve.

Each serving: About 375 calories, 18g protein, 47g carbohydrate, 12g total fat (3g saturated), 0mg cholesterol, 1,485mg sodium.

Soba Noodles Primavera with Miso

A quick and easy Asian-inspired pasta primavera made with packaged broccoli flowerets and shredded carrots. For a nutritional boost, we used soba noodles (Japanese buckwheat noodles) and miso (concentrated soybean paste).

PREP: 20 MINUTES   COOK: 20 MINUTES
MAKES 4 MAIN-DISH SERVINGS.

1 package (15 ounces) extrafirm
  tofu, rinsed, drained, and patted dry
1 package (8 ounces) soba noodles
1 tablespoon olive oil
1 medium red pepper, thinly sliced
1 large onion (12 ounces), sliced
2 garlic cloves, crushed with
  garlic press
1 tablespoon grated, peeled
  fresh ginger

1/4 teaspoon crushed red pepper
1 bag (16 ounces) broccoli flowerets,
  cut into 1 1/2-inch pieces
1 bag (10 ounces) shredded carrots
1/4 cup water
1/4 cup red (dark) miso paste
2 green onions, trimmed and thinly
  sliced

1. Cut tofu horizontally in half. Cut each half into 1-inch pieces; set aside.

2. In large saucepot, cook noodles as label directs.

3. Meanwhile, in nonstick 5- to 6-quart Dutch oven, heat oil over medium-high heat until hot. Add red pepper and onion and cook, stirring occasionally, until golden, about 10 minutes. Add garlic, ginger, crushed red pepper, and tofu; cook, stirring, 1 minute. Add broccoli, carrots, and water; heat to boiling over medium-high heat. Reduce heat to medium; cook, covered, until vegetables are tender, about 7 minutes.

4. Drain noodles, reserving 3/4 cup noodle water. Return noodles to saucepot.

5. With wire whisk, mix miso paste and reserved noodle water until blended. To serve, toss noodles with tofu mixture, green onions, and miso-paste mixture.

Each serving: About 455 calories, 26g protein, 68g carbohydrate, 11g total fat (2g saturated), 0mg cholesterol, 1,290mg sodium.

Broccoli Stir-fry with Rice Noodles

Inspired by our favorite Thai noodle dishes, this dish incorporates colorful fresh vegetables and herbs into a lime-spiked coconut sauce.

PREP: 30 MINUTES   COOK: 20 MINUTES   MAKES 4 MAIN-DISH SERVINGS.

3 limes
8 ounces dried flat rice noodles (about 1/4 inch wide)
2 tablespoons vegetable oil
1 bag (16 ounces) broccoli flowerets
3 medium carrots, peeled and each cut lengthwise in half, then crosswise into 1/4-inch-thick slices
2 heads baby bok choy (about 6 ounces each), cut crosswise into 1-inch-thick slices
1 cup light unsweetened coconut milk (not cream of coconut)

2 tablespoons brown sugar
3 tablespoons reduced-sodium soy sauce
2 tablespoons Asian fish sauce (see Tip page 57)
1/4 teaspoon crushed red pepper
3 garlic cloves, crushed with garlic press
1 tablespoon grated, peeled fresh ginger
1 cup loosely packed fresh basil and/or mint leaves, coarsely chopped

1. From limes, grate 1 teaspoon peel and squeeze 1/4 cup juice.

2. In large saucepot, heat *3 quarts water* to boiling over high heat; remove saucepot from heat. Place noodles in water; soak until softened, 6 to 8 minutes. Drain noodles; rinse under cold running water and drain again. Set aside.

3. Meanwhile, in deep nonstick 12-inch skillet, heat 1 tablespoon oil over medium-high heat until hot. Add broccoli, carrots, and *1/4 cup water;* cover and cook, stirring once or twice, until vegetables are tender-crisp, about 7 minutes. Add bok choy to skillet and cook, uncovered, just until vegetables are tender, 3 to 4 minutes. Transfer vegetables to bowl.

4. In small bowl, combine *2/3 cup water,* coconut milk, sugar, soy sauce, fish sauce, crushed red pepper, and lime juice; stir until blended.

5. In same skillet, heat remaining 1 tablespoon oil over medium-high heat until hot. Add garlic, ginger, and lime peel; cook, stirring, 30 seconds. Add coconut-milk mixture; heat to boiling. Stir in noodles and vegetables; heat through.

6. Transfer to warm serving bowl. Toss with basil and/or mint to serve.

Each serving: About 420 calories, 11g protein, 70g carbohydrate, 13g total fat (4g saturated), 0mg cholesterol, 1,215mg sodium.

Sesame Noodles

Sesame Noodles

A peanut butter and sesame dressing spiked with orange juice makes this Chinese restaurant–style pasta a favorite with kids as well as adults.

PREP: 15 MINUTES   COOK: 15 MINUTES
MAKES 6 MAIN-DISH SERVINGS.

1 package (16 ounces) spaghetti
1 cup fresh orange juice
1/4 cup seasoned rice vinegar
1/4 cup soy sauce
1/4 cup creamy peanut butter
1 tablespoon Asian sesame oil
1 tablespoon grated, peeled fresh ginger
2 teaspoons sugar
1/4 teaspoon crushed red pepper

1 bag (10 ounces) shredded carrots (about 3 1/2 cups)
3 Kirby cucumbers (about 4 ounces each), unpeeled and cut into 2" by 1/4" matchstick strips
2 green onions, trimmed and thinly sliced
2 tablespoons sesame seeds, toasted (optional)
green onions for garnish

1. In large saucepot, cook pasta as label directs.
2. Meanwhile, in medium bowl, with wire whisk or fork, mix orange juice, vinegar, soy sauce, peanut butter, oil, ginger, sugar, and crushed red pepper until blended; set aside.
3. Place carrots in colander; drain pasta over carrots. In large warm serving bowl, toss pasta mixture, cucumbers, and sliced green onions with peanut sauce. If you like, sprinkle pasta with sesame seeds. Garnish with green onions.

Each serving: About 445 calories, 15g protein, 76g carbohydrate, 9g total fat (2g saturated), 0mg cholesterol, 1,135mg sodium.

Eggplant Parmesan

If making our weeknight recipe, Pasta with Eggplant Sauce (page 137), stash 2 cups of the tomato sauce and a quarter of the casserole in the fridge to use with that recipe.

PREP: 1 HOUR PLUS STANDING   BAKE: 1 HOUR
MAKES 6 MAIN-DISH SERVINGS.

TOMATO SAUCE
1 tablespoon olive oil
1 medium onion, finely chopped
4 garlic cloves, minced
2 cans (28 ounces each) whole
   tomatoes in puree
1/4 cup tomato paste
1 teaspoon salt
1/4 teaspoon coarsely ground black
   pepper
1/4 cup loosely packed fresh basil
   leaves, chopped (optional)

EGGPLANT
3 medium eggplants (about 3 1/4
   pounds)
2 tablespoons olive oil
1/2 teaspoon salt

BREAD-CRUMB TOPPING
2 teaspoons butter or margarine
2 slices firm white bread, coarsely
   grated
1 garlic clove, minced
2 ounces part-skim mozzarella
   cheese, shredded (1/2 cup)
2 tablespoons freshly grated
   Parmesan cheese

CHEESE FILLING
1 container (15 ounces) part-skim
   ricotta cheese
2 ounces part-skim mozzarella
   cheese, shredded (1/2 cup)
2 tablespoons grated Parmesan
   cheese
1/4 teaspoon coarsely ground black
   pepper

1. Prepare tomato sauce: In 4-quart saucepan, heat oil over medium heat until hot. Add onion and cook, stirring occasionally, until tender, about 8 minutes. Add garlic and cook 1 minute longer, stirring frequently.

2. Stir in tomatoes with their puree, tomato paste, salt, and pepper, breaking up tomatoes with side of spoon; heat to boiling over high heat. Reduce heat to low and simmer, uncovered, until the sauce thickens slightly, about 25 minutes. Stir in basil, if using. Makes about 6 cups. (Cover and refrigerate 2 cups sauce to make Pasta with Eggplant Sauce, or save for another use).

3. While sauce is simmering, prepare eggplant: Preheat oven to 450°F. Grease 2 large cookie sheets. Trim ends from eggplants and discard. Cut eggplants lengthwise into 1/2-inch-thick slices. Arrange slices in single layer on cookie sheets. Brush top of eggplant slices with oil and sprinkle with salt.

4. Bake eggplant slices 25 to 30 minutes or until tender and golden, rotating sheets and turning slices over halfway through cooking; remove eggplant from oven and turn oven control to 350°F.

5. Prepare topping: In nonstick 10-inch skillet, melt butter over medium heat. Add grated bread and garlic, and cook, stirring occasionally, until lightly browned, about 7 minutes. Transfer to small bowl. Add mozzarella and Parmesan; toss until evenly mixed.

6. Prepare filling: In medium bowl, mix ricotta, mozzarella, Parmesan, and pepper until blended.

7. Assemble the casserole: Into 13" by 9" glass baking dish, evenly spoon 1 cup tomato sauce. Arrange half of eggplant, overlapping slices slightly, in baking dish. Top with 1 cup tomato sauce, then dollops of cheese filling. Top cheese with 1 cup tomato sauce, remaining eggplant, and remaining tomato sauce (about 1 cup). Sprinkle top with bread-crumb topping.

8. Cover baking dish with foil and bake 15 minutes. Remove cover and bake until hot and bubbly, about 15 minutes longer. Let stand 10 minutes for easier serving.

Each serving: About 380 calories, 21g protein, 35g carbohydrate, 21g total fat (10g saturated), 49mg cholesterol, 1,373mg sodium.

Spinach and Rice Frittata

Rice, spinach, and cottage cheese mixed up with mostly egg whites make a delicious, fluffy omelet dinner. Using leftover rice cuts down on prep time, but if you don't have any, cook ½ cup raw rice according to package directions.

PREP: 20 MINUTES   BAKE: 20 MINUTES
MAKES 4 MAIN-DISH SERVINGS.

2 teaspoons olive oil
1 medium onion, sliced
8 large egg whites (1 cup, see Tip page 148)
2 large eggs
1 package (10 ounces) frozen chopped spinach, thawed and squeezed dry

1½ cups leftover cooked long-grain white rice
1 container (8 ounces) low-fat cottage cheese (1%)
⅓ cup nonfat (skim) milk
¼ cup grated Romano cheese
½ teaspoon salt
⅛ teaspoon ground black pepper

1. Preheat oven to 425°F. In oven-safe nonstick 10-inch skillet (if skillet is not oven-safe, wrap handle with double layer of foil), heat oil over medium heat until hot. Add onion and cook, covered, until tender and golden, about 8 minutes, stirring occasionally.
2. Meanwhile, in large bowl, with fork, stir egg whites, whole eggs, spinach, rice, cottage cheese, milk, Romano, salt, and pepper until blended.
3. Stir egg mixture into onion in skillet and place in oven. Bake until frittata is set in center, 18 to 20 minutes. Cut into wedges to serve.

Each serving: About 265 calories, 23g protein, 25g carbohydrate, 7g total fat (2g saturated), 114mg cholesterol, 830mg sodium.

Egg and Black Bean Burritos

Scrambled eggs with a sprinkling of Monterey Jack are wrapped in flour tortillas with black beans and salsa—like the popular takeout but better—and it's on the table in just 15 minutes!

PREP: 10 MINUTES   COOK: 5 MINUTES
MAKES 4 MAIN-DISH SERVINGS.

1 can (15 to 19 ounces) black beans, rinsed and drained
1 jar (11 ounces) medium-hot salsa (about 1¹/₄ cups)
6 large eggs
¹/₄ teaspoon salt
¹/₈ teaspoon coarsely ground black pepper
4 ounces shredded Monterey Jack cheese (1 cup)
4 (10-inch) flour tortillas

1. In small microwave-safe bowl, mix black beans with salsa; set aside. In medium bowl, with wire whisk or fork, beat eggs, salt, and black pepper until blended.

2. Heat nonstick 10-inch skillet over medium-high heat until hot. Add egg mixture to skillet. As egg mixture begins to set around edge, stir lightly with heat-safe rubber spatula or wooden spoon to allow uncooked egg mixture to flow toward side of pan. Continue cooking until edges are set to desired doneness, about 5 minutes. Remove skillet from heat; sprinkle cheese evenly over eggs.

3. Meanwhile, in microwave oven, heat black-bean mixture on High, stirring once, until heated through, 1 to 2 minutes. Cover and keep warm.

4. Stack tortillas and place between 2 damp microwave-safe paper towels. In microwave oven, heat tortillas on High until warm, about 1 minute.

5. For each burrito, place one-fourth of scrambled eggs down center of 1 tortilla; top with about one-fourth of black-bean mixture. Fold two opposing sides of tortilla over filling, then fold over remaining sides to form a package.

Each serving: About 575 calories, 28g protein, 71g carbohydrate, 21g total fat (9g saturated), 344mg cholesterol, 1,550mg sodium.

Corn and Jack Quesadillas

Corn and Jack Quesadillas

After a bite of one of these quesadillas, you'll agree that taking the time to grill fresh ears of corn and then cut the kernels from the cob was well worth it. If you're grilling dinner the day before you serve these, you can grill the corn ahead and refrigerate it for even easier prep.

PREP: 10 MINUTES PLUS COOLING   GRILL: 11 MINUTES
MAKES 4 MAIN-DISH SERVINGS.

3 large ears corn, husks and silks removed
4 (8- to 10-inch) low-fat flour tortillas
4 ounces reduced-fat Monterey Jack cheese, shredded (1 cup)
1/2 cup mild or medium-hot salsa
2 green onions, trimmed and thinly sliced

1 head romaine lettuce, thinly sliced
1 tablespoon olive oil
1 tablespoon cider vinegar
1/2 teaspoon coarsely ground black pepper
1/4 teaspoon salt

1. Prepare grill.
2. Place corn on hot grill rack over medium-high heat. Cover grill and cook corn, turning frequently, until brown in spots, 10 to 15 minutes. Transfer corn to plate; set aside until cool enough handle. With sharp knife, cut kernels from cobs.
3. Place tortillas on work surface. Evenly divide Monterey Jack, salsa, green onions, and corn on half of each tortilla. Fold tortilla over filling to make 4 quesadillas.
4. Place quesadillas on hot grill rack. Grill quesadillas, turning once, until browned on both sides, 1 to 2 minutes. Transfer quesadillas to cutting board; cut each into 3 pieces.
5. In large bowl, toss romaine with oil, vinegar, pepper, and salt. Serve quesadillas with romaine salad.

Each serving: About 330 calories, 16g protein, 47g carbohydrate, 11g total fat (5g saturated), 20mg cholesterol, 940mg sodium.

Spinach and Corn Quesadillas

Fresh veggies, canned black beans, and spicy Jack cheese are layered between flour tortillas and then baked until deliciously crisp.

PREP: 30 MINUTES BAKE: 10 MINUTES
MAKES 4 MAIN-DISH SERVINGS.

1 can (15 to 19 ounces) black beans, rinsed and drained
1 tablespoon olive oil
1 medium onion, thinly sliced
1¼ cups corn kernels cut from cobs (2 ears)
1 garlic clove, crushed with garlic press

2 teaspoons chili powder
1 teaspoon ground cumin
⅛ teaspoon coarsely ground black pepper
1 bag (6 ounces) baby spinach leaves
8 (8-inch) flour tortillas
4 ounces shredded Monterey Jack cheese with jalapeño chiles (1 cup)

1. Preheat oven to 400°F. In small bowl, with fork or potato masher, mash 1 cup black beans until almost smooth. Set aside mashed and whole beans, separately.
2. In nonstick 12-inch skillet, heat oil over medium heat until hot. Add onion and cook, stirring occasionally, until tender and golden, 15 to 20 minutes. Add corn, garlic, chili powder, cumin, pepper, and whole beans and cook, stirring frequently, 2 minutes.
3. Increase heat to medium-high. Gradually add spinach to skillet, stirring until spinach has wilted and water has evaporated, about 3 minutes.
4. Spread mashed beans on 1 side of 4 tortillas (mashed beans will be dry and pasty and will not cover the entire tortilla); place, bean side up, on large cookie sheet. Top with equal amounts of spinach mixture and sprinkle with cheese. Place remaining tortillas on top of filling.
5. Bake quesadillas until tortillas are crisp, cheese has melted, and filling is heated through, 8 to 10 minutes. Cut into wedges to serve.

Each serving: About 665 calories, 26g protein, 100g carbohydrate, 22g total fat (9g saturated), 30mg cholesterol, 1,180mg sodium.

Savory Tomato Tart

A dramatically beautiful main dish. For more color, we included a yellow tomato, but it's equally delicious with all red.

PREP: 45 MINUTES   BAKE/BROIL: 30 MINUTES
MAKES 6 MAIN-DISH SERVINGS.

Pastry for 11-inch Tart (page 71)
1 tablespoon olive oil
3 medium onions, thinly sliced
1/2 teaspoon salt
1 package (31/2 ounces) goat cheese
1 ripe medium yellow tomato (8 ounces), cut into 1/4-inch-thick slices

2 ripe medium red tomatoes (8 ounces each), cut into 1/4-inch-thick slices
1/2 teaspoon coarsely ground black pepper
1/4 cup Kalamata olives, pitted and chopped

1. Preheat oven to 425°F. Prepare Pastry for 11-Inch Tart as recipe directs. On lightly floured surface, with floured rolling pin, roll dough into 14-inch round. Ease dough into 11" by 1" round tart pan with removable bottom. Fold overhang in and press dough against side of pan so it extends 1/8 inch above rim. With fork, prick dough at 1-inch intervals. Line tart shell with foil; fill with pie weights or dry beans. Bake 15 minutes. Remove foil with weights. Bake until golden, 5 to 10 minutes longer. If the shell puffs up during baking, gently press it down with back of spoon.
2. Meanwhile, in nonstick 12-inch skillet, heat oil over medium heat until hot. Add onions and 1/4 teaspoon salt; cook, stirring frequently, until very tender, about 20 minutes.
3. Turn oven control to Broil. Spread onions over bottom of tart shell and crumble half of goat cheese on top. Arrange yellow and red tomatoes, alternating colors, in concentric circles over onion-cheese mixture. Sprinkle with remaining 1/4 teaspoon salt and pepper. Crumble remaining goat cheese on top of tart.
4. Place tart on rack in broiling pan. Place pan in broiler about 7 inches from heat source. Broil until cheese has melted and tomatoes are heated through, 6 to 8 minutes. Sprinkle with olives.

Each serving: About 420 calories, 8g protein, 33g carbohydrate, 29g total fat (15g saturated), 54mg cholesterol, 755mg sodium.

Tomato and Cheese Pie

Tomato and Cheese Pie

A savory custard pie that bakes right in the pie plate—with no crust!

PREP: 20 MINUTES   BAKE: 35 MINUTES
MAKES 6 MAIN-DISH SERVINGS.

1 container (15 ounces) part-skim
  ricotta cheese
4 large eggs
1/4 cup freshly grated Parmesan
  cheese
3/4 teaspoon salt plus additional for
  sprinkling
1/8 teaspoon coarsely ground black
  pepper plus additional for sprinkling

1/4 cup low-fat milk (1%)
1 tablespoon cornstarch
1 cup packed fresh basil leaves,
  chopped
1 pound ripe tomatoes (about
  3 medium), thinly sliced

1. Preheat oven to 375°F. In large bowl, with wire whisk or fork, beat ricotta, eggs, Parmesan, salt, and pepper until blended.

2. In cup, with fork, stir milk and cornstarch until blended; whisk into cheese mixture. Stir in basil. Pour mixture into 9-inch glass or ceramic pie plate. Arrange tomatoes on top, overlapping if necessary. Sprinkle tomatoes with salt and pepper.

3. Bake pie until lightly browned around edge and center is puffed, 30 to 35 minutes.

Each serving: About 190 calories, 15g protein, 10g carbohydrate, 10g total fat (5g saturated), 167mg cholesterol, 515mg sodium.

Tofu and Vegetable Stir-fry

Choose extrafirm tofu so it won't fall apart during stir-frying. Spoon the saucy tofu-and-vegetable mixture over fragrant jasmine rice. Because the stir-fry takes only 20 minutes to cook, start the rice as soon as you step into the kitchen.

PREP: 15 MINUTES   COOK: 20 MINUTES
MAKES 4 MAIN-DISH SERVINGS.

1 cup jasmine rice
4 teaspoons vegetable oil
1 package (16 ounces) extrafirm tofu, patted dry and cut into 1" by 1/2" pieces
2 tablespoons reduced-sodium soy sauce
8 ounces (half 16-ounce bag) broccoli flowerets
1 medium red pepper, cut into 1/2-inch pieces

1 cup water
2 tablespoons Asian fish sauce (see Tip page 57)
2 tablespoons grated, peeled fresh ginger
1 tablespoon brown sugar
1 tablespoon cornstarch
1 large garlic clove, crushed with garlic press
1 bag (10 ounces) shredded carrots
3 tablespoons fresh lime juice

1. Prepare jasmine rice as label directs; keep warm.
2. Meanwhile, in nonstick 12-inch skillet, heat 2 teaspoons oil over medium-high heat until hot. Add tofu and 1 tablespoon soy sauce and cook, stirring frequently (stir-frying) but gently, until heated through and golden, about 5 minutes. Transfer tofu to plate; set aside.
3. In same skillet, heat remaining 2 teaspoons oil. Add broccoli and red pepper and cook, covered, stirring occasionally, until vegetables are tender-crisp, about 6 minutes.
4. In small bowl, with fork, mix water with fish sauce, ginger, brown sugar, cornstarch, garlic, and remaining 1 tablespoon soy sauce.
5. Return tofu to skillet and add carrots. Stir soy-sauce mixture to blend and add to skillet; heat to boiling. Boil, gently stirring, 1 minute. Stir in lime juice. Serve over rice.

Each serving: About 425 calories, 19g protein, 61g carbohydrate, 11g total fat (1g saturated), 0mg cholesterol, 1,020mg sodium.

Grilled Tofu and Veggies

Shake things up for nonmeat eaters with a barbecue surprise: tender tofu, zucchini, and pepper with a great hoisin-ginger glaze. Be sure to buy extrafirm tofu; other varieties will fall apart while cooking.

PREP: 25 MINUTES   GRILL: 12 MINUTES
MAKES 4 MAIN-DISH SERVINGS.

HOISIN GLAZE
- 1/3 cup hoisin sauce
- 2 garlic cloves, crushed with garlic press
- 1 tablespoon vegetable oil
- 1 tablespoon reduced-sodium soy sauce
- 1 tablespoon grated, peeled fresh ginger
- 1 tablespoon seasoned rice vinegar
- 1/8 teaspoon ground red pepper (cayenne)

TOFU AND VEGGIES
- 1 package (15 ounces) extrafirm tofu
- 2 medium zucchini (about 10 ounces each), each cut lengthwise into quarters, then crosswise in half
- 1 large red pepper, cut lengthwise into quarters, stem and seeds discarded
- 1 bunch green onions, trimmed
- 1 teaspoon vegetable oil

1. Prepare glaze: In small bowl, with fork, mix hoisin sauce, garlic, oil, soy sauce, ginger, vinegar, and ground red pepper until well blended.

2. Prepare grill.

3. Prepare tofu and veggies: Cut tofu horizontally into 4 pieces, then cut each piece crosswise in half. Place tofu on paper towels; pat dry with additional paper towels. Spoon half of hoisin glaze into medium bowl; add zucchini and red pepper. Gently toss vegetables to coat with glaze. Arrange tofu on large plate and brush both sides of tofu with remaining glaze. On another plate, rub green onions with oil.

4. Place tofu, zucchini, and red pepper on hot grill rack over medium heat. Cook tofu, gently turning once with wide metal spatula, 6 minutes. Transfer tofu to platter; keep warm. Continue cooking vegetables until tender and browned, about 5 minutes longer, transferring them to platter with tofu as they are done. Add green onions to grill during last minute of cooking time; transfer to platter.

Each serving: About 245 calories, 15g protein, 22g carbohydrate, 11g total fat (1g saturated), 0mg cholesterol, 615mg sodium.

Japanese Eggplant and Tofu Stir-fry

Japanese eggplant is long and slender, with tender flesh and bright purple skin. When cooked, the eggplant absorbs the wonderful flavor of the stir-fry sauce. Serve with brown rice to enjoy it all.

PREP: 25 MINUTES   COOK: 20 MINUTES
MAKES 4 MAIN-DISH SERVINGS.

1 pound firm tofu, drained and cut into 1-inch cubes

1 cup vegetable broth

1/4 cup reduced-sodium soy sauce

2 tablespoons brown sugar

2 tablespoons cornstarch

2 tablespoons vegetable oil

4 medium Japanese eggplants (about 4 ounces each), cut diagonally into 2-inch-thick pieces

8 ounces shiitake mushrooms, stems removed, and caps cut into quarters

1 tablespoon grated, peeled fresh ginger

3 garlic cloves, crushed with garlic press

3 green onions, trimmed and thinly sliced

2 heads baby bok choy (about 6 ounces each), cut crosswise into 1-inch slices

1. In medium bowl, place 3 layers paper towel; add tofu and cover with 3 more layers paper towel, pressing gently to extract liquid from tofu. Let tofu stand 10 minutes to drain.

2. Meanwhile, in small bowl, with fork, mix *1/2 cup water,* broth, soy sauce, sugar, and cornstarch until blended; set aside.

3. In deep, nonstick 12-inch skillet or wok, heat 1 tablespoon oil over medium-high heat until hot. Add eggplant and *1/3 cup water;* cover and cook, stirring occasionally, until eggplant is tender, 7 to 10 minutes. Transfer eggplant to small bowl; set aside.

4. Add remaining 1 tablespoon oil to skillet and heat until hot. Add mushrooms and tofu and cook, stirring frequently (stir-frying), until tofu is lightly browned, about 5 minutes. Stir in ginger, garlic, and half of green onions; cook, 1 minute, stirring. Add bok choy and cook, stirring occasionally, until vegetables are lightly browned, about 4 minutes longer.

5. Stir vegetable-broth mixture to blend; add broth mixture and eggplant to tofu mixture. Heat to boiling over medium-high heat; reduce heat to low and simmer, stirring, 1 minute. Sprinkle with remaining green onions before serving.

Each serving: About 280 calories, 15g protein, 33g carbohydrate, 13g total fat (1g saturated), 0mg cholesterol, 865mg sodium.

Moroccan-Spiced Sweet Potato Medley

A spicy combination of vegetables cooked with bulgur and sweetened with dark raisins.

PREP: 20 MINUTES   COOK: 30 MINUTES
MAKES 4 MAIN-DISH SERVINGS.

2 teaspoons olive oil
1 medium onion, sliced
2 garlic cloves, crushed with garlic press
1 1/2 teaspoons ground coriander
1 1/2 teaspoons ground cumin
1 teaspoon salt
1/4 teaspoon ground red pepper (cayenne)
1 1/2 pounds sweet potatoes (about 2 medium), peeled and cut into 3/4-inch pieces

1 can (14 1/2 ounces) stewed tomatoes
1 cup bulgur (cracked wheat)
2 1/4 cups water
1 can (15 to 19 ounces) garbanzo beans, drained and rinsed
1/2 cup dark seedless raisins
1 cup loosely packed fresh cilantro leaves, chopped
plain low-fat yogurt (optional)

1. In nonstick 12-inch skillet, heat oil over medium heat until hot. Add onion and cook, covered, stirring occasionally, until tender and golden, about 8 minutes. Add garlic, coriander, cumin, salt, and ground red pepper and cook, stirring, 1 minute.

2. Add the potatoes, tomatoes, bulgur, and water; heat to boiling over medium-high heat. Reduce heat to medium-low; cover and simmer until potatoes are fork-tender, about 20 minutes. Stir in beans, raisins, and cilantro; heat through. Serve with yogurt, if you like.

Each serving: About 525 calories, 16g protein, 109g carbohydrate, 5g total fat (1g saturated), 0mg cholesterol, 1,080mg sodium.

Moroccan-Spiced Sweet-Potato Medley

Grilled Tomato and Basil Pizzas

Grilled Tomato and Basil Pizzas

Garden tomatoes and basil make a wonderful topping for pizza cooked over the coals. For the crust, use frozen bread dough or fresh dough from the supermarket or pizzeria.

PREP: 30 MINUTES   GRILL: 6 TO 9 MINUTES PER PIZZA
MAKES 4 PIZZAS OR 4 MAIN-DISH SERVINGS.

1 pound (1 piece) frozen bread
    dough, thawed (from 2- to 3-pound
    package)
2 tablespoons olive oil
4 ripe medium tomatoes (about 1 1/2
    pounds), sliced
4 ounces fresh mozzarella cheese,
    sliced, or 1 cup shredded Fontina
    cheese

1/2 teaspoon salt
1/2 teaspoon ground black pepper
1 cup loosely packed fresh basil
    leaves, chopped, plus additional
    leaves for garnish

1. Prepare grill.

2. Cut thawed bread dough into 4 pieces. On oiled cookie sheet, spread and flatten 1 piece of dough to 1/8-inch thickness. Lightly brush dough with some oil. On same cookie sheet, repeat with another piece of dough. Repeat with another oiled cookie sheet and remaining pieces of dough. For easiest handling, cover and refrigerate dough on cookie sheets until ready to use.

3. Place 1 piece of dough at a time, greased side down, on grill over medium-low heat. Grill until dough stiffens (dough may puff slightly) and grill marks appear on underside, 2 to 3 minutes. Brush top with some oil.

4. With tongs, turn crust over. Quickly top with one-fourth of tomatoes and one-fourth of cheese. Cook pizza until cheese melts and underside is evenly browned and cooked through, 4 to 6 minutes longer.

5. With tongs, transfer pizza to cutting board. Sprinkle pizza with 1/8 teaspoon salt and 1/8 teaspoon pepper. Scatter one-fourth of chopped basil on pizza and garnish with basil leaves. Drizzle with some oil, if you like. Serve immediately.

6. Repeat with remaining dough and toppings.

Each serving: About 495 calories, 18g protein, 63g carbohydrate, 20g total fat (7g saturated), 34mg cholesterol, 1,175mg sodium.

Whole-Wheat Pita Pizzas with Vegetables

Whole-Wheat Pita Pizzas with Vegetables

We topped whole-wheat pitas with ricotta cheese, garbanzo beans, and sautéed vegetables for a fast dinner the whole family will love.

Prep: 25 minutes   Bake: 13 minutes
Makes 8 pizzas or 4 main-dish servings.

1 teaspoon olive oil
1 medium red onion, sliced
2 garlic cloves, crushed with garlic press
1/4 teaspoon crushed red pepper
8 ounces broccoli flowerets, cut into 11/2-inch pieces
1/2 teaspoon salt
1/4 cup water

1 can (15 to 19 ounces) garbanzo beans, rinsed and drained
1 cup part-skim ricotta cheese
4 (6-inch) whole-wheat pitas, split horizontally in half
1/2 cup freshly grated Parmesan cheese
2 medium plum tomatoes, cut into 1/2-inch pieces

1. Preheat oven to 450°F. In nonstick 12-inch skillet, heat oil over medium-high heat until hot. Add onion and cook, stirring occasionally, until golden, 7 to 10 minutes. Add garlic and crushed red pepper, and cook, stirring, 30 seconds. Add broccoli flowerets, 1/4 teaspoon salt, and water; heat to boiling. Reduce heat to medium and cook, covered, until broccoli is tender-crisp, about 5 minutes.

2. Meanwhile, in small bowl, with potato masher or fork, mash beans with ricotta and remaining 1/4 teaspoon salt until almost smooth.

3. Arrange pita halves on 2 large cookie sheets. Bake until lightly toasted, about 3 minutes. Spread bean mixture on toasted pitas. Top with broccoli mixture and sprinkle with Parmesan. Bake until heated through, 7 to 10 minutes longer. Sprinkle with tomatoes to serve. Serve 2 rounds per person.

Each serving: About 510 calories, 27g protein, 77g carbohydrate, 13g total fat (6g saturated), 27mg cholesterol, 1,155mg sodium.

South-of-the-Border Vegetable Hash

A savory combination of classic hash ingredients (without the meat) gets a new flavor twist from kidney beans, cilantro, and fresh lime.

PREP: 20 MINUTES   COOK: 30 MINUTES
MAKES ABOUT 8 CUPS OR 4 MAIN-DISH SERVINGS.

3 large Yukon Gold potatoes (about 1½ pounds), cut into ¾-inch pieces
2 tablespoons olive oil
1 large onion (12 ounces), cut into ¼-inch pieces
1 medium red pepper, cut into ¼-inch-wide strips
3 garlic cloves, crushed with garlic press

2 teaspoons ground cumin
¾ teaspoon salt
1 can (15 to 19 ounces) red kidney or black beans, rinsed and drained
2 tablespoons chopped fresh cilantro
plain yogurt, lime wedges, salsa, and toasted corn tortillas (optional)

1. In 3-quart saucepan, combine potatoes and enough *water* to cover; heat to boiling over high heat. Reduce heat to low; cover and simmer until potatoes are almost tender, about 5 minutes. Drain well.

2. Meanwhile, in nonstick 12-inch skillet, heat oil over medium-high heat until hot. Add onion, red pepper, garlic, cumin, and salt and cook, stirring occasionally, 10 minutes. Add drained potatoes and cook until vegetables are lightly browned, 5 minutes longer. Stir in beans and cook until heated through, about 2 minutes longer. Sprinkle with chopped cilantro.

3. Serve vegetable hash with yogurt, lime wedges, salsa, and corn tortillas, if you like.

Each serving without accompaniments: About 360 calories, 12g protein, 63g carbohydrate, 8g total fat (1g saturated), 0mg cholesterol, 625mg sodium.

Shortcut Asparagus Pizzas

You won't find this delicious pie—with shiitake mushrooms and asparagus topping—at your local pizzeria.

PREP: 30 MINUTES   BAKE: 20 MINUTES
MAKES 2 PIZZAS OR 4 MAIN-DISH SERVINGS.

1 1/2 pounds asparagus, trimmed
1 tablespoon olive oil
1 large onion (12 ounces), cut in half and thinly sliced
1/4 pound shiitake mushrooms, stems removed and caps thinly sliced
1 large garlic clove, minced
1/2 teaspoon salt
1/4 teaspoon ground black pepper

1/4 cup water
1 pound (1 piece) frozen bread dough, thawed (from 2- to 3-pound package)
4 ounces Fontina cheese, shredded (1 cup)
2 tablespoons freshly grated Parmesan cheese

1. Preheat oven to 425°F.

2. If using thin asparagus, cut each stalk crosswise in half; if using medium asparagus, cut stalks into 1 1/2-inch pieces. In nonstick 12-inch skillet, heat oil over medium-high heat until hot. Add onion and mushrooms and cook, stirring often, until vegetables are tender and golden, 8 to 10 minutes. Add asparagus, garlic, salt, pepper, and water; cover and cook until asparagus is tender-crisp, about 5 minutes longer. Remove skillet from heat.

3. Cut dough in half. On greased cookie sheet, spread and flatten 1 piece of dough to 1/8-inch thickness (about 10 inches in diameter). Pinch edges of dough to form rim. Repeat with another greased cookie sheet and remaining piece of dough. Sprinkle 1/2 cup Fontina over each piece of dough, then spread with equal amounts of vegetable mixture. Sprinkle each with 1 tablespoon Parmesan.

4. Bake pizzas on 2 oven racks until crust is lightly browned and cheese melts, 18 to 20 minutes, rotating cookie sheets between upper and lower racks halfway through baking.

Each serving: About 505 calories, 22g protein, 66g carbohydrate, 18g total fat (7g saturated), 36mg cholesterol, 1,230mg sodium.

Polenta with Spicy Eggplant Sauce

A great dinner you can whip up after you get home from work: Polenta cooks in the microwave oven with minimal attention while you prepare a quick skillet sauce.

PREP: 15 MINUTES   COOK: 25 MINUTES
MAKES 4 MAIN-DISH SERVINGS.

1 tablespoon olive oil
1 medium onion, finely chopped
2 small eggplants (about 1 pound each), cut into 1-inch pieces
1 garlic clove, crushed with garlic press
1/4 teaspoon crushed red pepper

1 can (28 ounces) crushed tomatoes
1 1/2 teaspoons salt
2 cups low-fat (1%) milk
1 1/2 cups yellow cornmeal
Parmesan-cheese wedge for garnish (optional)

1. In nonstick 12-inch skillet, heat oil over medium heat until hot. Add onion and cook, stirring occasionally, 5 minutes. Increase heat to medium-high; add eggplant and cook, stirring occasionally, until golden and tender, about 8 minutes. Add garlic and crushed red pepper and cook, stirring, 1 minute. Add tomatoes, 1/2 teaspoon salt, and *1/2 cup water;* heat to boiling. Reduce heat to low; cover and simmer, stirring occasionally, 10 minutes.

2. Meanwhile, in deep 4-quart microwave-safe bowl or casserole, combine milk, cornmeal, 1 teaspoon salt, and *4 1/2 cups water*. Cook in microwave oven on High until thickened, 15 to 20 minutes. After the first 5 minutes of cooking, whisk vigorously until smooth (mixture will be lumpy at first), and twice more during remaining cooking time.

3. While polenta is cooking, with vegetable peeler, remove long, thin strips from Parmesan wedge for garnish, if you like.

4. To serve, spoon polenta into 4 bowls; top with eggplant sauce. Garnish each serving with some Parmesan strips if using.

Each serving: About 380 calories, 13g protein, 71g carbohydrate, 6g total fat (2g saturated), 5mg cholesterol, 1,235mg sodium.

Polenta with Spicy Eggplant Sauce

Polenta Bake with Butternut Squash

We top ready-made polenta with a creamy mixture of butternut squash and Parmesan cheese for an easy weeknight dinner.

PREP: 30 MINUTES   BAKE: 15 MINUTES
MAKES 4 MAIN-DISH SERVINGS.

1 log (24 ounces) precooked polenta
4 teaspoons olive oil
1 jumbo onion (1 pound), cut into
   1/4-inch pieces
2 garlic cloves, crushed with
   garlic press
1 bag cut-up butternut squash
   (11/4 pounds)
11/4 cups low-fat milk (1%)

2 teaspoons cornstarch
1/2 teaspoon salt
1/8 teaspoon coarsely ground
   black pepper
6 tablespoons freshly grated
   Parmesan cheese plus additional
   for serving
1/2 cup loosely packed fresh basil
   leaves, chopped

1. Preheat oven to 450°F. Cut polenta log crosswise in half, then cut each half lengthwise into 4 slices. In lightly greased 8" by 8" ceramic or glass baking dish, place 6 slices polenta. Cut remaining 2 slices into 1/4-inch pieces; set aside.

2. In nonstick 12-inch skillet, heat oil over medium-high heat until hot. Add onion and garlic, and cook, stirring occasionally, 5 minutes. Add squash; cover and cook, stirring occasionally, until vegetables are tender and lightly browned, about 15 minutes longer.

3. Meanwhile, bake polenta slices in baking dish until heated through, about 10 minutes.

4. In small bowl with fork, stir milk, cornstarch, salt, pepper, and 4 table-spoons Parmesan until well combined. Add milk mixture to skillet; heat to boiling over medium-high heat. Reduce heat to low; cook, stirring occasionally, 2 minutes.

5. Spoon squash mixture over polenta slices; top with polenta pieces and remaining 2 tablespoons Parmesan. Bake until heated through, about 5 minutes. Sprinkle with basil before serving. Serve with additional Parmesan, if you like.

Each serving: About 350 calories, 12g protein, 60g carbohydrate, 8g total fat (3g saturated), 9mg cholesterol, 1,005mg sodium.

Mushroom and Barley Pilaf

A mixture of fresh and dried mushrooms and hearty root vegetables are cooked with barley for a flavorful entrée—especially good on a crisp autumn day!

PREP: 20 MINUTES PLUS STANDING   COOK: 50 MINUTES
MAKES 9 CUPS OR 4 MAIN-DISH SERVINGS.

1 package (about 1/2 ounce) dried
  porcini mushrooms (about 1/2 cup)
2 tablespoons butter or margarine
1 medium onion, finely chopped
2 medium carrots, peeled and each
  cut lengthwise in half, then
  crosswise into 1/4-inch-thick slices
2 medium parsnips (about 6 ounces
  each), peeled and each cut
  lengthwise in half, then crosswise
  into 1/4-inch-thick slices

2 packages (about 4 ounces each)
  sliced wild mushroom blend or 8
  ounces mixed wild mushrooms,
  tough stems removed and caps
  thinly sliced
1 1/4 teaspoons salt
1/4 teaspoon coarsely ground
  black pepper
1/4 teaspoon dried thyme
1 1/2 cups pearl barley (about
  12 ounces)
1/2 cup loosely packed fresh parsley
  leaves, chopped

1. In medium bowl, pour *3 cups boiling water* over porcini mushrooms; let stand 10 minutes. With slotted spoon, remove porcini, reserving liquid. Rinse porcini to remove any grit, then coarsely chop and set aside. Strain mushroom liquid through sieve lined with paper towels into liquid measuring cup. Add enough *water* to liquid to equal 4 1/2 cups total; set aside.

2. Meanwhile, in nonstick 5- to 6-quart Dutch oven or saucepot, melt butter over medium-high heat. Add onion, carrots, parsnips, wild mushrooms, salt, pepper, and thyme and cook, stirring occasionally, until vegetables are tender-crisp, about 10 minutes.

3. Add barley and porcini with soaking liquid; heat to boiling. Reduce heat to medium-low; cover and simmer, stirring occasionally, until barley and vegetables are tender, 35 to 40 minutes. Stir in parsley.

Each serving: About 425 calories, 12g protein, 82g carbohydrate, 10g total fat (4g saturated), 16mg cholesterol, 837mg sodium.

Eggplant and Spinach Stacks

Layering thick slices of roasted eggplant with spinach, zucchini, and cheese is a fun, new way to serve this sometime forgotten vegetable!

PREP: 25 MINUTES   ROAST: 30 MINUTES
MAKES 4 MAIN-DISH SERVINGS.

1 medium eggplant (about 1 1/2 pounds)
1 tablespoon plus 3 teaspoons olive oil
1 teaspoon salt
2 garlic cloves, crushed with
 garlic press
1/8 teaspoon crushed red pepper
1 small zucchini (about 6 ounces),
 trimmed and coarsely shredded

1 bag (6 ounces) baby spinach leaves
1 cup part-skim ricotta cheese
1/4 cup freshly grated Parmesan cheese
2 plum tomatoes, seeded and cut into
 paper-thin strips
1/8 teaspoon cracked black pepper

1. Preheat oven to 450°F. Trim ends from eggplant and discard. Cut eggplant crosswise into 8 rounds of equal thickness. Brush cut sides of eggplant slices with 1 tablespoon plus 2 teaspoons oil and sprinkle with 1/2 teaspoon salt.

2. In 15 1/2" by 10 1/2" jelly-roll pan, arrange slices in single layer. Roast, carefully turning slices halfway through cooking, until tender and golden, 20 to 25 minutes.

3. Meanwhile, in nonstick 12-inch skillet, heat remaining 1 teaspoon oil over medium-high heat until hot. Add garlic and red pepper and cook, stirring, 30 seconds. Add zucchini and 1/4 teaspoon salt and cook, stirring, 2 minutes. Gradually add spinach to skillet, stirring until spinach has wilted and water has evaporated, about 3 minutes; set aside.

4. In small bowl, with fork, mix ricotta, Parmesan, and remaining 1/4 teaspoon salt until blended.

5. Remove eggplant from oven. Mound spinach mixture on 4 of the larger eggplant slices; top with remaining eggplant slices. Mound equal amounts of cheese mixture on each eggplant stack. Return to oven and heat through, about 5 minutes (cheese will melt over side of stacks).

6. With wide metal spatula, transfer stacks to 4 dinner plates. Top with tomatoes and sprinkle with black pepper to serve.

Each serving: About 230 calories, 13g protein, 17g carbohydrate, 14g total fat (5g saturated), 23mg cholesterol, 795mg sodium.

INDEX

METRIC CONVERSION CHARTS

The recipes that appear in this cookbook use the standard United States method for measuring liquid and dry or solid ingredients (teaspoons, tablespoons, and cups). The information on this chart is provided to help cooks outside the U.S. successfully use these recipes. All equivalents are approximate.

METRIC EQUIVALENTS FOR DIFFERENT TYPES OF INGREDIENTS

A standard cup measure of a dry or solid ingredient will vary in weight depending on the type of ingredient. A standard cup of liquid is the same volume for any type of liquid. Use the following chart when converting standard cup measures to grams (weight) or milliliters (volume).

Standard Cup	Fine Powder (e.g. flour)	Grain (e.g. rice)	Granular (e.g. sugar)	Liquid Solids (e.g. butter)	Liquid (e.g. milk)
1	140 g	150 g	190 g	200 g	240 ml
3/4	105 g	113 g	143 g	150 g	180 ml
2/3	93 g	100 g	125 g	133 g	160 ml
1/2	70 g	75 g	95 g	100 g	120 ml
1/3	47 g	50 g	63 g	67 g	80 ml
1/4	35 g	38 g	48 g	50 g	60 ml
1/8	18 g	19 g	24 g	25 g	30 ml

USEFUL EQUIVALENTS FOR LIQUID INGREDIENTS BY VOLUME

1/4 tsp	=					1 ml
1/2 tsp	=					2 ml
1 tsp	=					5 ml
3 tsp	=	1 tbls	=		1/2 fl oz	=	15 ml
		2 tbls	=	1/8 cup	=	1 fl oz	=	30 ml
		4 tbls	=	1/4 cup	=	2 fl oz	=	60 ml
		5 1/3 tbls	=	1/3 cup	=	3 fl oz	=	80 ml
		8 tbls	=	1/2 cup	=	4 fl oz	=	120 ml
		10 2/3 tbls	=	2/3 cup	=	5 fl oz	=	160 ml
		12 tbls	=	3/4 cup	=	6 fl oz	=	180 ml
		16 tbls	=	1 cup	=	8 fl oz	=	240 ml
		1 pt	=	2 cups	=	16 fl oz	=	480 ml
		1 qt	=	4 cups	=	32 fl oz	=	960 ml
						33 fl oz	=	1000 ml	= 1 l

USEFUL EQUIVALENTS FOR DRY INGREDIENTS BY WEIGHT

(To convert ounces to grams, multiply the number of ounces by 30.)

1 oz	=	1/16 lb	=	30 g
4 oz	=	1/4 lb	=	120 g
8 oz	=	1/2 lb	=	240 g
12 oz	=	3/4 lb	=	360 g
16 oz	=	1 lb	=	480 g

USEFUL EQUIVALENTS FOR COOKING/OVEN TEMPERATURES

	Fahrenheit	Celsius	Gas Mark
Freeze Water	32° F	0° C	
Room Temperature	68° F	20° C	
Boil Water	212° F	100° C	
Bake	325° F	160° C	3
	350° F	180° C	4
	375° F	190° C	5
	400° F	200° C	6
	425° F	220° C	7
	450° F	230° C	8
Broil			Grill

USEFUL EQUIVALENTS FOR LENGTH

(To convert inches to centimeters, multiply the number of inches by 2.5.)

1 in	=		2.5 cm
6 in	=	1/2 ft =	15 cm
12 in	=	1 ft =	30 cm
36 in	=	3 ft = 1 yd =	90 cm
40 in	=		100 cm = 1 m